The 3rd Power

The 3rd Power

THE FAITH FORMULA TO SOOTHE THE
SOUL AND RESTORE THE SPIRIT

Scott W. Ventrella

CrossLink Publishing

CrossLink Publishing
1601 Mt. Rushmore Rd, STE 3288
Rapid City, SD 57702

Ordering Information:
Quantity sales. Special discounts are available on quantity purchases by corporations, associations, and others. For details, contact the "Special Sales Department" at the address above.

The 3rd Power/Ventrella —1st ed.

First edition: 10 9 8 7 6 5 4 3 2 1

ISBN: 978-1-63357-181-5

Library of Congress Control Number: 2019943139

Scripture quotations marked "AKJV" are take from the Holy Boble, King James Version, (1769 edition of the 1611 Authorized Version) (Public Domain).

Scripture quotations marked "BSB" are taken from The Holy Bible, Berean Study Bible, BSB, Copyright ©2016, 2018 by Bible Hub. Used by Permission. All Rights Reserved Worldwide.

Scripture quotations marked "CSB" are taken from the Christian Standard Bible, Copyright © 2017 by Holman Bible Publishers. Used by permission. Christian Standard Bible®, and CSB® are federally registered trademarks of Holman Bible Publishers, all rights reserved.

To the memory of my mom, Jane Isabelle Romano Ventrella, who taught me the faith— not only by her words, but even more so through her actions.

2/25/1929 – 6/23/2018

Contents

Acknowledgements

This book has been many years in the making. Though only one name appears on the cover, many have helped me along the way—thus, exemplifying "We Power" at its best. Two people, in particular, played crucial roles from start to finish. A very special thank you to MeiMei Fox and Eileen Burke for providing editorial assistance, particularly in the early days. Their ideas and insights helped shape the book, which proceeded through many iterations over time. In addition to their editorial work, they both shared their talents as gifted and accomplished writers. Their input was invaluable.

When writing the final manuscript, I decided to forego re-reading or proofing the work. I was concerned it would slow me down and lead me to overthink and overwrite every sentence and paragraph. As a result, I decided to hand the work over to a professional copy editor. Thanks to my friend and literary agent, Patti DeMatteo, I was introduced to Joe Kraynak. Joe assisted on many different fronts—everything from formatting and organizing to clarifying thoughts and concepts. He was a pleasure to work with and helped me cross the finish line and deliver a final manuscript in presentable form. I'm grateful for his help.

I am especially thankful for friends and acquaintances who agreed to be interviewed as I was developing the core ideas and content for the book. (I don't think they knew what they were getting themselves into!) The following people generously shared their own faith walk and provided me with input and feedback on the material: Suzanne Douglas-Harris, Kristen Hoban, Tehri Gasparrini, Kate Jacullo, and John Papa.

Though they were unaware of it at the time, up to that point, I had been relying on "Me Power" and found myself in "stuck" mode. Conducting the interviews provided much needed outside inspiration and clarity of thought and direction. With that outside help, I was able to get back on track.

Thanks also to Rick Bates, Managing Editor of CrossLink Publishing, and his staff for believing in the potential of this book to change lives.

The writing process is long and arduous, punctuated with a series of highs and lows. During the low periods, I found encouragement from two very close friends — Deanna Brown and Jack Navarro. Somehow, they knew when I needed a friend the most. I can't thank them enough.

Of course, my wife, Catherine, and our kids, Jennifer and Andrew, are a constant source of support and encouragement, providing the impetus for all I do. They're my reason.

Finally, I thank Almighty God, "Thee Power," for His guidance throughout this process. I am eternally grateful. It is my hope that this work has glorified His name.

The Power of Faith—Believe in Unseen Potential

A re you feeling heavy? If so, you're not alone. With all the bad news swirling around it's easy to grow despondent and anxious. But as Christians, we have no reason to be all doom and gloom. We have been given the great gift of faith, particularly faith in Jesus Christ who came to us as the light of the world:

> When Jesus spoke again to the people, he said, "I am the light of the world. Whoever follows me will never walk in darkness, but will have the light of life" (John 8:12 NIV).

With 24/7 news coverage streaming to our TVs, computers, and smart phones, along with the constant and often heated commentary and discussion via social media, becoming pre-occupied (if not obsessed) with the latest news cycle is far too easy. Thank God we have an option; we can tune out all the bad news and tune in to the Good News provided by our Christian faith. Jesus promised "new life" and salvation for those who believe and follow Him. He gave us the Holy Spirit to guide us through difficult times, leading us to a peace "which surpasses all understanding." Christians who are committed to, and practice, *authentic* Christianity can rejoice in knowing that "those who hope in the

Lord will renew their strength. They will soar on wings like eagles; they will run and not grow weary, they will walk and not be faint" (Isaiah 40:31 NIV).

Since the dawn of time, people have been proclaiming that the end of the world is near. In fact, some of Jesus' own disciples, as well as many of the early Christians, believed that His return would occur within their lifetimes, bringing the end of the world with it. Given the current state of affairs in our world, many people feel certain that we are living our last days and that Armageddon (the final battle between good and evil prior to Judgment Day) is imminent.

Regardless of whether or not you believe in Doomsday, few would argue that we are living in a time when the world has become an increasingly terrifying and overwhelming place. The nightly news is akin to a horror movie—except for the fact that the blood, gore, and mayhem are real. Here is just a small sampling of the events taking place around the world, in our country, and in our homes:

- School shootings across the country, including the Sandy Hook Elementary School massacre in Newtown, Connecticut, where 26 were killed (20 of whom were children), and Stoneman Douglas High School in Parkland, Florida killing 17 students.
- Suicide bomber kills 22 people, mostly young children, attending an Ariana Grande concert in Manchester, England.
- Terrorists using a car and knives attack people on the London Bridge, killing seven, wounding many more.
- Increasing attacks on Christians around the world, killing 7,000 last year alone according to Open Doors USA, an international organization that tracks and brings awareness to Christian persecution. The killings have been brutal, afflicting young and old alike. On Easter Sunday in 2019, suicide bombers killed hundreds of innocent people in a

series of six coordinated attacks in Sri Lanka. Three of the bombs were detonated in Christian houses of worship.

- Closer to home, a gunman opened fire on a crowd of concertgoers on the Las Vegas Strip, killing 58 people and injuring more than 850 others.
- On Easter Sunday, 2017, 74-year-old Robert Goodwin was shot and killed by a man for no apparent reason, who filmed and streamed the killing to Facebook Live and later took his own life.
- Other acts of violence shared on social media include sexual assault, murder, and suicide. A 12-year-old girl in Georgia recorded her own suicide by hanging via the Live. me app.
- The suicide rate in America is at a 30-year high.
- Death by opioid overdose is at epidemic proportions—49,068 deaths in the U.S. in 2017 alone. In that same year, the number of deaths involving all drugs exceeded 72,000.

In addition, people are struggling with job insecurity, economic instability, shrinking medical benefits, an aging population, and increasingly hostile public discourse. Finally, a widespread sense of disillusionment with government and politics, corporations, marriage, the public education system, the church, and other formerly reliable institutions prevails. As a result, people are feeling anxious, insecure, and fearful with a bleak view of their future. As one Millennial put it, "The world has gone off the deep end. We've seen better times."

A Perplexing Paradox

On 9/11, my friend Bridget was working at the World Trade Center on the 95th floor of the South Tower. As she was checking her voicemail, she suddenly heard the loud whine of an airplane.

Looking up, she saw it hit the North Tower. Along with many of her colleagues, she decided to exit the building, immediately via the stairs.

While on her way down, at approximately the 54th floor, the second plane hit her building. In that moment, she knew without a doubt that they were under attack.

Bridget expected panic to ensue. But instead, she noticed that most of the people making their way down the long, dark staircase were calm. Most were praying, saying The Lord's Prayer or "Hail Mary" under their breaths. Although she believed in God, she rarely prayed and said she "didn't pay God much attention." But in that moment, she turned to God for comfort. She prayed the entire way to the ground floor.

As she exited the building, Bridget saw bodies hitting the ground. Emergency personnel told her not to look around—the surrounding scene was too gruesome.

Only moments after she was whisked to safety, her building collapsed. Ninety of her coworkers died that day.

The horror of her experience on 9/11 brought Bridget back to faith, as it did for many other people. I witnessed a surge in attendance at noon Mass that day. Normally, I would see about 30 people in church; that day, the church was jam-packed, with over 150 people in attendance! The following Sunday, the pews were filled again. People across the country flocked to houses of worship. They were shaken back to their faith. My dad, a World War II veteran, used to say, "There's no such thing as an atheist in a foxhole."

In especially dark periods of history—during wars and famines, economic downturns such as the Great Depression, and pandemics—people have turned to their faith in God for comfort and reassurance. Given the trouble the world is experiencing today, you would think that people would once again turn toward faith for solace and hope. Think again. Amazingly, Christianity in America is in sharp decline. Consider the following statistics based on a survey conducted by the Pew Research Center:

- The percentage of adults who describe themselves as Christian has dropped by close to eight percentage points in seven years to 71%.
- Over the same period, the number of those not affiliated with a religion has jumped from 16% to 23%.
- Among the non-affiliated, 31% include atheists, agnostics (doubters), and those who don't believe in anything in particular.

The 3rd Power

For this reason, I have felt *called* to write this book. Simply put, *The 3rd Power* is a message to all Christians—including those in name only, seekers who are new to Christ's teachings, and those who have fallen completely away from religion—to deepen their faith.

People need God now more than ever. But instead of moving closer to Him, they are distancing themselves from and abandoning their faith. To be clear, it is *they* who are abandoning God; it is *not* God who is abandoning them. People lose faith and stray from formal religion for many reasons—a growing mistrust of religious institutions; hypocritical behavior on the part of so-called Christians; a culture that glorifies wealth, power, and beauty; a chaotic world that can make God seem distant, uncaring, and uninvolved; or simply a bad case of complacency or apathy.

Recently, I was running with my friend, Matt, who had been out of work for quite a long spell. He finally landed a job in New York City. Knowing he was a Christian, I asked him how his faith in God had helped him through the many months of unemployment.

"Actually, I decided that I no longer needed God in my life," Matt replied. "I realized that I could handle my life just fine without His help. And as you can see, all is good."

A colleague of mine said something similar to me one morning over coffee. "I don't need to go to a building with incense and candles every week to worship God. I can experience Him while hiking in the woods or fishing on a lake."

Clearly, we can experience God through nature—after all, He created it! But worshipping the creation instead of the Creator can actually distance us from God and weaken our understanding and appreciation of how God works with us and through us to attain fulfillment and bring His Kingdom to fruition. Without religion, we can experience some level of spirituality in nature, but we lose the framework of scripture study, prayer, and worship that helps us maintain alignment with the Divine.

Of course, religion can drive a wedge between us and God, unintentionally or intentionally. Well-meaning, but poorly prepared, church leadership may inadvertently drive people from the church by failing to engage the congregation and provide for members' spiritual needs. Worse, throughout history, religion has been abused and misused for self-service instead of for the service of God and His people, giving the word "religion" negative connotations for many people. Those who corrupt religion for their own gain perform a great disservice to true believers by pushing them away from formal faith practices and communal worship. Unfortunately, many people have a tendency to "throw the baby out with the bathwater"—to dismiss *all* religion simply because, in their limited experience, they have not yet found a congregation that meets their needs and suits their tastes.

We need to keep in mind that Jesus was deeply religious. He and His family were devout Jews who followed all the rituals and practices of the faith. At the same time, even He was wary of the so-called religious leaders of His time, namely the Pharisees and the Sadducees. He knew greed and hatred lurked in their hearts and warned His apostles that these men of the cloth were actually wolves in sheep's clothing.

When I introduce this book to friends and family, their first question usually is, "So, what is the *third power?*" My answer: "*The 3ʳᵈ Power* is a simple yet powerful way to think about and apply our faith to address all kinds of challenges, as well as the opportunities that come our way."

The 3ʳᵈ Power is based upon three distinct, yet interrelated, components:

Me Power ⟶ *We Power* ⟶ *Thee Power*

The following sections briefly explain each of these three components.

Me Power

Me Power is the innate, divine power that God has instilled in each of us. It includes our unique gifts, talents, and strengths—everything that makes us who we are, including our personality. At first glance, Me Power seems like an incredibly selfish notion, especially considering that we are currently raising the selfie generation and living in an era where "it's all about me." But Me Power does not imply that a person is egotistical.

Me Power recognizes and acknowledges that God placed a bit of divinity in each one of us at the time of creation. As such, each of us has unique characteristics—special talents and gifts. Think of this as the inherent capability God expects us to develop and use to achieve self-fulfillment, make the world a better place, and glorify Him.

This, of course, is easier said than done. Many of us are living in a spiritual fog; our senses dulled due to a lack of commitment to our Christian faith. Me Power is a call to recommit through regular *inward* examination—spending time and energy in a prayerful, contemplative mode versus living mostly outside of ourselves, focused on other people, achievements, social media, and things. The more we are distracted by outward interests, the more we lose touch with the Kingdom of God within.

Several years ago, I was working with a senior rabbi to help develop his leadership skills. One day, I received an important call from the president of the synagogue seeking advice on a very serious matter involving the rabbi.

She told me she had discovered that he had plagiarized sermons over the years—not just a sentence or paragraph or two, but complete sermons. He had delivered and even published them as his own! I couldn't believe that a spiritual leader would do something so antithetical to the teachings of his faith. What was so perplexing is that he was a very talented rabbi with a special gift for connecting with people through his faith-filled sermons. In my estimation, he didn't need to lift someone else's work. He apparently did not recognize his own God-given talent, or didn't trust it.

All too often, we look to others to solve our problems or tackle important tasks. We see this in children who expect their parents to settle an argument with a sibling or friend. We see it in older kids who ask a friend or parent to write a paper for them or prepare a college essay. We see it in the workplace when coworkers seek out others to do a job they were assigned to complete. Yet, many times, it serves us best to take on something difficult or at least work together with another person to overcome a challenge, rather than delegating our personal responsibility entirely. This is how we learn new skills and how we grow.

As *the* role model for Christians, Jesus was both God and fully human. As a human being, He had an acute awareness and understanding of His own gifts and unique talents. One of these was a knack for persuading people to follow Him. Convincing the twelve Apostles to abandon their families and livelihoods to join His cause couldn't have been easy. But He was a gifted storyteller, using parables—often with an unusual twist—to capture the imaginations and hearts of would-be followers. He also was skilled at debating, passionate about His vision and mission, and never intimidated by people of power and wealth. Jesus was a master at connecting, inspiring, and encouraging others with a message of hope and salvation. These are just a handful of the qualities that enabled Him to carry out His mission.

Me Power requires that we conduct a humble assessment of our unique characteristics, both good and bad. The one important exception in Jesus' case is that because He was also fully God, He had no faults. He was not born with original sin and never would sin. Therefore, he did not have to concern Himself with identifying quirks or deficiencies in His thoughts and behavior. As mere mortals, we not only have to assess our spiritual gifts, but also come to terms with our faults and weaknesses and work, with God's help, to minimize or eliminate them altogether.

We Power

We Power recognizes that we live interdependent lives. As our Christian faith tells us, we are all connected as one part of the same body—the Body of Christ. We Power is an outward power.

At times, we are compelled to reach out to others for guidance, support, and consolation. Other times, we are called to support and encourage others, especially when they are going through a rough time. Given my background in career counseling, friends and acquaintances often approach me seeking help in career transitions and networking.

Once again, we see this power most exemplified by the life of Jesus, particularly during the years of his public ministry. He healed the sick, restored sight to the blind, made the lame walk, and raised the dead. He made himself totally available to others in need. As a human being, He also needed comfort and support. Most poignantly, when entering the Garden of Gethsemane, he asked His three closest friends—Peter, James, and John—to accompany Him. He knew He was about to enter His darkest moment where all sins—past, present, and future—would be revealed to Him. Yes, the fully human Jesus recognized the need for consolation and encouragement.

Some people have a difficult time with We Power—especially those who have a strong, independent streak. They may have a "go-it-alone" mentality driven by pride. Relying solely or primarily on Me Power, this personality type often has a limited impact by failing to leverage the power of others. This is especially well-illustrated with young children who want to express their independence by crossing the street by themselves when they still require guidance from someone older and wiser. But adults can be just as strong-willed, too stubborn to ask for help even when they desperately need it.

Jesus provided the perfect example of We Power in action. When the time came to spread the Word, he recruited and trained the twelve apostles and sent them to surrounding towns to cover more ground. After his death, the surviving apostles carried on His work on earth and, over the course of time, by leveraging We Power, have spread the Good News around the world!

Thee Power

Thee Power is the ultimate power. It is our direct connection to God, independent of all others. It's a connection we can make through many different methods—prayer, meditation, and contemplation being the primary ones. Supplemental methods include attending religious services, engaging in Bible study, and reading scripture and inspirational books.

All three Powers have one common denominator: God.

Understanding these three distinct yet interrelated Powers is the key to deepening your faith. Think of Me, We, and Thee Powers as *believing* and *trusting* in ourselves, others, and God. The key to a deeper faith is understanding when and how to bring all three together in the proper proportion. For instance, some of us are very good at using Me Power when needed but don't give much thought to We or Thee Power. Others overlook Me Power and rely on We Power. Still, others shift all the responsibility to Thee Power while sitting around waiting for God to solve their problems without lifting a hand to help themselves.

Brenda, a 48-year-old mother of four young children, was diagnosed with stage 4 colon cancer. The news devastated her, as well as her friends and family.

Instead of giving into fear and despondency, she tapped into the 3rd Power. Exercising her Me Power, she conducted research to learn about the disease and possible treatments. She changed her diet and developed a new exercise regimen. To harness We Power, Brenda started a blog to keep her friends and family updated on her condition and to ask for their prayers and support. She maintained Thee Power throughout the ordeal through prayer and daily worship.

I suspect you think this story will have a happy ending. It does not. Brenda succumbed to the disease just shy of her 50th birthday. This might lead you to ask, "What's the point, then?"

The point is that Brenda did everything she could to beat the cancer, employing her full individual, community, and faith powers. This enabled her to stay upbeat, connected, and loving throughout her battle with her disease.

Although she couldn't live forever (none of us can), Brenda was able to make the best of the limited time she had left on earth to grow closer to those around her and to have a positive impact on them by demonstrating peaceful contentment right up to the end.

Many people fall away from their faith and stop believing in God altogether when faced with such a tragedy. But during Brenda's eulogy, her husband, Bill, spoke about the numerous people who had asked him, "How could this have happened to such a wonderful, faithful family? Where was God in all of this?" Bill said he wanted everyone to know that God had been with them every step of the way. He had not abandoned them.

That was four years ago. I have stayed in close touch with Bill ever since, and not once has he expressed bitterness toward God.

On the contrary, he has drawn even closer to God. That doesn't mean that he and his children don't still grieve or feel the emptiness of Brenda's loss—they do. But as he has shared with me during our many conversations, "Life on earth is not the end." He has taken the eternal view. Brenda lives on.

One of the problems with contemporary Christianity is that the ideas of sin, suffering, and death have been all but removed from the equation. Many Christians are attracted to the "feel good" aspects of the faith, also known as the "prosperity gospel." The idea is that God only wants us to be happy, healthy, and wealthy. Some Christian preachers go as far as saying that hell does not exist. Increasingly, in our "live and let live" culture, some believe that Christians should not only tolerate abhorrent behavior but also consider it morally acceptable. Among certain contemporary Christians, the idea of sin is outdated/outmoded; its only purpose was to keep people in check by threatening eternal punishment with fire and brimstone.

Of course, God doesn't want us to be miserable, but when we look to Christ as our role model, we see that He experienced suffering and death. He accepted it as a part of a bigger picture, as I discuss in Chapter 7. Sin, suffering, and death cannot be whitewashed over and dismissed. They are an inextricable part of life itself and much of the reason we practice religion—to minimize sin and suffering and overcome death through eternal life. That is why it is so important for us Christians to reacquaint ourselves with what it means to be Christian.

The 3rd Power is a means for deepening our faith, which will certainly make life smoother here on earth while compelling us to fully develop and maximize the use of the abundant gifts God has bestowed upon us. More importantly, it helps us prepare for the life that follows. Jesus did not promise a blissful life on earth should we decide to follow Him. Rather, He said that He was the

Way to the Father and through Him we might all have eternal life.

PART 1

Me Power

God placed a bit of divinity in each one of us at the time of creation. As such, each of us has unique characteristics—special talents and gifts. Me Power is the sum total of these talents and gifts, which God expects us to develop in order to achieve our full potential.

To fully achieve Me Power, we must develop a greater awareness of the Divine within us. We must strive to become more spiritual beings, learn how to take control of our thoughts, and commit to doing what's right—to follow the example Jesus set for us.

In this part, you discover how to

- Assess and achieve spiritual fitness
- Evaluate and change your thinking to improve your actions and outcomes
- Define your platinum standard and use it as your moral compass

CHAPTER 1

Spiritual Fitness

Me Power recognizes and acknowledges that God placed a bit of divinity in each of us at the time of creation. We were made in His image. The term also recognizes that each of us has unique characteristics—special talents and spiritual gifts. Think of what makes you unique as your inherent capability, which God expects you to tap into and use for the good of humanity. This is well illustrated in "The Parable of the Talents" (Matthew 25:14–30). I'll paraphrase here but strongly suggest you look it up and read it for yourself. In the parable, Jesus tells of a master who, upon leaving for a trip, gives each of his three servants a quantity of "talents" based on each servant's ability to invest wisely. When the master returns, he learns that two of the servants had doubled his investment through prudent trading. This greatly pleased the master who rewarded them with greater responsibility (more talents).

I should mention here that a talent at that time represented the largest unit of currency. For instance, the largest sum given to one of the servants was five talents of either gold or silver, which was of enormous value at the time. Unfortunately, the third servant decided to protect the one talent he was entrusted with, burying it in the ground for safekeeping. When the servant presented the single talent to his master, the master was enraged.

He expected a return on his investment. As a result, he took back what little the servant had and gave it to the others.

Jesus used this as a metaphor for us, referring not to gold or silver, but talent in the modern sense of the word: "a *natural* ability or aptitude." As in the parable, we're expected to put our talents to good use. This, of course, is easier said than done. It presumes that we're conscious of the divinity within and aware of our unique talents. Unfortunately, many people are living in a "spiritual fog." Their senses have been dulled due to a lack of commitment to their Christian faith—a commitment that (among other things) includes a regular *inward* examination of faith. Many have been neglectful in this area and then wonder why their faith has grown stale and dull. There's a simple explanation for this.

Internal Warfare

Just as we have been instilled with the Divine, we all have "a touch of the gutter," (as James Cagney, one of the great actors of the twentieth century, once stated). That is, we have the stain of original sin. The internal warfare then is the battle between the good and the evil that goes on everyday within us. You've seen this depicted many times on TV and in the movies as an angel and a devil sitting on opposite shoulders. The angel appears on one shoulder encouraging us to avoid temptation and do the right thing. On the opposite shoulder is the devil telling us to "go for it —it's not wrong. In fact, it's good for you!"

Our inclination to do good or evil comes from whom we choose to listen to internally—the angel (divine) or devil (original sin)—and what we choose to pay attention to externally—the positive influences and the opportunities to do good or the temptations to do evil. The more we listen to the devil within us and shift our attention to the temptations around us, the farther we stray from God and good.

As we stray from God, we soon forget about the divinity within us. We no longer think to look for God in the most obvious and nearest place—inside ourselves.

According to an old Hindu legend, at one time, everyone on earth was a god, but they so sinned and abused the Divine that Brahma, god of all gods, decided to take away the godhead and hide it where people would never find it. "We will bury it deep in the earth," said the other gods. "No," said Brahma, "because humans will dig down in the earth and find it." "Then we will sink it in the deepest ocean," they said. "No," said Brahma, "because humans will learn to dive and find it there too." "We will hide it on the highest mountain," they said. "No," said Brahma, "because humans will someday climb every mountain on earth and again capture the godhead." "Then we do not know where to hide it where they cannot find it," said the lesser gods. "I will tell you," said Brahma, "Hide it deep within each person. They will never think to look there." And that is what they did.

It's time to take an inward look.

The Spiritual Fitness Assessment

Doctors generally recommend that to maintain proper health we have an annual physical exam, regardless of whether or not we're sick. As part of the exam, the doctor checks vital signs such as blood pressure, heart rate, and temperature. Routine blood work is conducted as well. The older we get, the more important these annual check-ups become. Now, if we have a tendency to skip the annual physical, we may find ourselves in serious trouble. In a sense, it's like disconnecting an early warning system. Being proactive and facilitating early detection are smart, sensible ways to manage our health.

Subjecting yourself to an annual spiritual exam is even more important because your spiritual well-being impacts every aspect of your life on earth—physical health, relationships, education, career, and so forth. And it extends into the hereafter when your spiritual being outlives your physical being.

I encourage you to start your search for God in the closest place you will find Him—within you. Take the following "Spiritual Fitness Assessment" to evaluate three key areas relating to Me Power:

- Faith commitment
- Faith practices
- Faith activation

Faith Commitment

Your faith commitment is a measure of your dedication to the Christian faith. It's an assessment of how committed you are in the following three areas:

- Living a life of faith—both in word and in deed
- Following Jesus Christ
- Practicing your faith 24/7, 365 days a year

I think it's fair to say that most Christians do not choose Christianity. Rather, it is chosen for us by well-meaning parents or surrogates such as grandparents or caregivers. My own adoption of faith started with baptism, which I received a few months after I was born. This was followed by first communion and eventually confirmation. Of course, attending weekly church services was routine. When I was growing up, my parents would herd the seven of us into the family station wagon every Sunday to drive to the local church for Sunday mass. Back then we would dress in formal attire—jacket and tie for the boys (the tie was a clip on) with freshly polished shoes and dresses and hats for the girls. How my parents were able to accomplish getting us to church on time is beyond my comprehension—just short of a miracle! In the Ventrella household, religious practices were mandatory.

That meant church every week and catechism throughout the school year. Back then, religious education continued right up through twelfth grade. As my older siblings reached high school, attending religious education classes on Monday evenings was definitely not cool. They would push back, but my parents would have none of it.

I can still hear my dad saying (actually, hollering), "As long as you live in my house you will go to mass and attend religious education!" I mention this to make a point that, in my experience, faith was forced on me and my siblings. I can't speak for everyone in my family, but having religion forced upon us clearly caused some resentment. Faith equated to weekly mass, religious education, and prayer before meals. When we were young, dad would admonish us to "brush our teeth and say our prayers" before going to bed. Mom would usually slip into our bedroom and recite The Lord's Prayer. As Catholics, we had a Bible which was prominently displayed in a bookcase. To the best of my knowledge, it sat there—untouched and unread. I want to be very clear here lest there be any misunderstanding. This may sound like an indictment against my parents or the Catholic Church. It is not. My parents did what all good Christian parents do; they made sure we all had a foundation in faith. Additionally, they did their best to set a good example for us in their day-to-day actions. What they could not do (and no parent could do, for that matter) was to make a commitment to Jesus Christ on our behalf.

I recognized this limitation while raising our own children. My wife, Catherine, and I did our best to lay a faith foundation. This included weekly mass, religious education, receiving the sacraments, and prayer before meals and before bedtime. Every night, the four of us would gather in one of the kid's bedrooms, hold hands, and say prayers. We'd end each nightly prayer session with the question, "What are you most happy about today?" Each one of us would then describe at least one event or experience that we were grateful to God for. And, yes, attending weekly mass was mandatory in our house regardless of age. The one difference from when I was growing up was that religious education (at least in my parish) ended after being confirmed in the ninth grade.

As a catechist preparing young adults for confirmation for the past thirty years, I've noticed that in these contemporary times, not only do formal religion classes end in the ninth grade, but so does weekly mass attendance. In the minds of many parents, as well as their kids, faith-based practices end at confirmation. The irony is that confirmation is not the end; it is just the beginning! The confirmed become full, active members of the church, giving them even greater responsibilities to participate and engage with their community of faith.

With our kids, we insisted on family participation that extended well beyond confirmation. That is, until our oldest, Jennifer, reached her senior year in high school. Any parent with kids in high school knows that the demands on their time grow with each passing year—academics, sports, social events, work, etc. They also become much more independent. It was through this combination of factors that one day Jennifer decided to dig in her heels. We were getting ready to go to mass one Saturday afternoon when she said she couldn't go because she had a babysitting job. I responded by saying, "Okay, then you can go tomorrow." To which she replied, "No, I'm not going tomorrow either. I'm too busy." That's when I turned into my father, shouting, "As long as you live in this house, you'll go to church!"

She didn't say anything. Instead, she went up to her room. I was fairly angry at the time thinking, "How can she defy me like that?"

Later that evening, I had an epiphany. I realized I was forcing faith on our daughter. I failed to see her as an independent young woman who was mature enough to make her own decisions about faith and religion. I went up to her room, knocked on the door and asked if I could come in. I told her I was wrong.

THE 3RD POWER • 25

I explained that just as my parents had done, we provided a solid foundation while she and Andrew were growing up. It was now up to her to make her own commitment—or not. Further, I said that although she was always welcome to join us, she was no longer required to attend mass. A few years later, when Andrew was a senior, I shared the same message. I should point out that Catherine and I were on the same page. In fact, she was less strict than I due to her upbringing. Her parents were not religious and did not go to church. (That's not to say that they weren't Christians or did not espouse and model positive values.) She came to a commitment in the Christian faith on her own as a college student. Several years later, she received confirmation and joined the Catholic Church.

I share this with you to illustrate that we all have different journeys to the Christian faith. Some are indoctrinated at a very young age—willingly or unwillingly. Others come to faith later in life. Regardless of which road you've traveled, what's critical is the extent to which you have made a personal commitment to follow Jesus Christ. After all, that's what it means to be a Christian—committing to and following in the footsteps of Jesus. Regardless of denomination (Catholic, Methodist, Baptist, Lutheran, etc.), all Christians share the same core beliefs. In short, Jesus Christ is the Son of God who lived on earth for a short time teaching us about the Father. He suffered an agonizing death as atonement for our sins and was resurrected three days later. For all Christians, He is our savior. He is the way, the truth, and the life. It is only through Him that we can live in eternity with our Father in heaven.

Types of Christians

One way to gauge your level of faith commitment is to consider what kind of Christian you are. I've identified three categories: *casual*, *Sunday*, and *committed*.

Casual Christians, or *"CHINO's (Christians in name only)* are believers but see and practice their faith in an ad hoc fashion; they identify as Christians but are lukewarm in the faith. They may sometimes attend church or not at all. In fact, many casual Christians hold the belief that they do not have to practice religion at all to be Christian. As the saying goes, who needs "bells and smells" to practice their Christian faith? Others attend services but only occasionally and usually when convenient. In my own Catholic faith, some attend Mass only twice a year: Christmas and Easter. They're often referred to as "Cheasters!"

Prayer is often on an as-needed basis—when they're in trouble, in times of need, or they don't know what else to do. The Bible is something to be seen and heard but not read.

I realize that this may sound as though I'm being critical—that's not my intention. Instead, I share this as an observation. The "casuals" are well-intentioned and do their best to live a decent life. The good news is that they do believe but in my view are missing out on what is literally a once in a lifetime opportunity to experience the full richness of the Christian faith.

Sunday Christians are exactly that—once-a-week Christians. They are Christian in name but attend church mostly out of a feeling of obligation or as a venue for socializing. The Sunday Christian often reverts to the Monday atheist. I say this mostly tongue in cheek, but I have known many Christians who check their Christianity at the door when going to work, driving in traffic, shopping, traveling, blogging, and attending sporting events. The behavior of some Christian parents at their child's soccer games reminds me of scenes from *The Exorcist*.

Regarding the Sunday Christian, their faith simply hasn't taken root. As Jesus himself stated in the "Parable of the Sower" (Matthew 13) picking up at Verse 18:

> Listen then to what the parable of the sower
> means: When anyone hears the message about

the kingdom and does not understand it, the evil one comes and snatches away what was sown in their heart. This is the seed sown along the path. The seed falling on rocky ground refers to someone who hears the word and at once receives it with joy. But since they have no root, they last only a short time. When trouble or persecution comes because of the word, they quickly fall away. The seed falling among the thorns refers to someone who hears the word, but the worries of this life and the deceitfulness of wealth choke the word, making it unfruitful. But the seed falling on good soil refers to someone who hears the word and understands it. This is the one who produces a crop, yielding a hundred, sixty or thirty times what was sown (Matthew 13:18-23).

Finally, *committed Christians* actively practice their faith 24/7, 365 days of the year. They have made the commitment to follow Jesus, internalizing His message and incorporating it into every aspect of life. Picking up at Matthew 13:23 (NIV), Jesus says, "But the seed falling on good soil refers to someone who hears the word and understands it. This is the one who produces a crop, yielding a hundred, sixty, or thirty times what was sown."

Jesus wants and expects us all to be committed in our faith—lukewarm is unacceptable.

Keep in mind that committed Christians are not perfect. In fact, they're sinners like all of us. They slip up, fall down, are prone to greed, envy, lust, anger, and every other human foible. The difference is they repent—they sincerely feel and express regret and remorse for their wrongdoing—knowing that sincere repentance will not be spurned by God, because Jesus has atoned for our sin. All we need to do is accept this amazing grace and continuously strive to live our faith—24/7 365 days a year!

Rate Yourself

How Would You Rate Yourself in Each Area of Faith Commitment?

Living a life of faith—both in word and in deed

1	2	3	4	5
Poor		Average		Excellent

Following Jesus Christ

1	2	3	4	5
Poor		Average		Excellent

Practicing your faith 24/7 - 365 days a year

1	2	3	4	5
Poor		Average		Excellent

Tips for Strengthening Your Faith Commitment

- If you have not already done so, commit your life to Jesus Christ. This can be done privately through a simple, yet earnest statement of faith such as, "Dear Jesus, I believe in You and commit my life to You. From here forward, I will do my best to follow you and live my life according to Christian principles."

- Honestly review the type of Christian you are: casual, Sunday only, or committed. Depending on your designation, introduce change gradually yet consistently to develop and maintain new habits.
- Place visual cues to remind yourself each and every day of your commitment. This could include anything from a religious piece of jewelry you wear to an inspirational message posted on your refrigerator or computer to a daily reminder "pushed" to your smartphone.

Faith Practices

Faith practices are a measure of how regularly you engage in formal religious activities, such as the following:

- Prayer
- Reading scripture and inspirational material
- Attending religious services and faith-based events

Of course, this is not an exhaustive listing. You may have other formal, faith-based activities you regularly engage in, such as going on spiritual retreats, having pitch-ins with fellow church members, or participating in regular Bible study.

Prayer

Committed Christians make a point to incorporate prayer into their daily lives. In Part 3 of this book, I discuss the many different types, forms, and methods of prayer, both formal and informal. For the purposes of assessing your spiritual fitness, think about how often you pray and under what circumstances.

Do you pray only when you need something or are in trouble?

Awhile back, I was talking to a close friend who had "found Jesus" as a younger man. He had become a changed person and lived his life as a true Christian. Somewhere along the line, I noticed a gradual shift away from his faith and I pointed it out to him. When pressed, he acknowledged as much and told me, "My faith (and prayer life) is like a bicycle. I only use it when I need it; otherwise, I simply put it away."

I felt bad for my friend. He eventually drifted completely away from his faith. He locked it up like a bicycle in a storage shed gathering dust and letting it rust. His life changed as well—and not for the better. Over time, he was beset with all kinds of problems; failing health, bankruptcy, foreclosure, and eventually divorce.

No, God did not punish him, but when we turn away or distance ourselves from God, we cut ourselves off from divine power and guidance. Strong faith requires daily, in fact, unceasing prayer. We are always in need, regardless of whether we realize it.

Scripture and Inspirational Material

Reading scripture and inspirational material are also very important faith practices. As previously mentioned, though we had a Bible growing up, I don't ever remember anyone reading it. Over 100 million Bibles are sold each year worldwide, with American consumers accounting for about 25 million copies. It's the best-selling publication in history. Unfortunately, few people actually *read* it. According to a new study conducted by the American Bible Society, 88% of the respondents own a Bible, but the majority (57%) read it only four times a year or less.

I didn't start reading the Bible until I was about 21 years old. I was in college at the time and a member of the college radio station, WXCI. One of my fellow disc-jockeys, Keith, had become a born-again Christian. Unlike other born-again Christians I've encountered, he was not pushy or "in-your-face." That didn't mean that he didn't feel compelled to bring other people to Christ. He adopted a more stealth-like approach. One subtle way he accomplished this was by leaving a pocket-sized, paperback Gideon's Bible in a prominent place at the station. This particular Bible included the New Testament with only two books from the Old Testament—Psalms and Proverbs.

I really didn't pay much attention to it at first, but one day my curiosity was piqued. I picked it up and opened to the first page where Keith had inscribed the following message: "To members of the WXCI staff as a Spirit booster."

I started to leaf through it stopping now and then to read passages. Each time I visited the station, I would do the same thing— open it to a random page and read. Of course, I did this only when no one else was around. God forbid someone should catch me reading the Bible! Silly of course but it was a function of age—I had a bit of a hippie streak in me and didn't want people to think I was going pure. In fairly short order, I had become engrossed in it and couldn't put it down. Finally, I decided to borrow it, so I could spend more time reading. I brought it home and eventually became more disciplined by reading it from beginning to end, starting with Matthew's Gospel right through Revelations and finally onto Proverbs and Psalms. I kept it by my bedside where reading it eventually became a habit. I was informally furthering my education on Jesus's life, death, and resurrection. Even though I didn't understand some parables at first, during subsequent readings I would have an incredible "aha" experience with complete understanding. The Holy Spirit was clearly at work.

A few years later, someone gave me a complete Bible—Old and New Testaments, which, over a long period of time, I read from cover to cover. I must admit, the Old Testament was a struggle to get through, some books very understandable and others very difficult. You may have had the same experience, but don't let that deter you. I strongly suggest that if you haven't yet, you develop the habit of reading scripture on a regular (if not daily) basis.

As St. Paul reminds us, "All Scripture is breathed out by God and profitable for teaching, for reproof, for correction, and for training in righteousness, that the man of God may be complete, equipped for every good work" (2 Timothy 3:16–17 NIV).

Many other sources of inspirational reading besides the Bible are readily available (although none can come close to the inspired word of God). Throughout history, excellent books have been written, both fiction and non-fiction, by religious figures as well as laypeople. Though I will refrain from endorsing any particular book or author, I urge you to be careful in your selection process. Some of the material can be misleading, actually moving you away from God and toward a false idol.

I offer the following guidance when looking for sources of inspiration outside of the Bible:

First and foremost, ask God to help you discern and direct you to "approved" literature.

Next, when reading reviews and perusing the table of contents, be sure that the author is moving you *towards* Jesus versus themselves. I recently read a non-fiction inspirational book for Christians, which several friends were raving about—a must read, according to them. Indeed, the book had numerous references to Jesus and scripture, but throughout, the author spoke about himself and his numerous experiences traveling the world. He detailed the exotic places he visited, luxurious hotels he stayed in, and exquisite restaurants he dined in. In my mind, he dwelled too much on his own success instead of pointing the reader to Jesus. As John the Baptist declared when his followers inquired about "the Christ," "He must increase, but I must decrease" (John 3:30 ESV). He realized it wasn't about him, but Jesus.

Finally, reading material should not contradict scripture—especially with regard to non-fiction. With fictional works, authors have more creative license, but these works may be misleading. Back in 2006, *The Da Vinci Code* made a huge splash but also stirred plenty of controversy. The problem was that the novel mixed historical fact with fiction that created confusion among its readers.

Somewhat more recently, *The Shack*, which was a highly popular work of fiction, pushed the boundaries of literary license. Professor Timothy Beal of Case Western University argues that the popularity of *The Shack* suggests that evangelicals might be shifting their theology. He cites the "non-biblical metaphorical models of God" in the book, as well as its "nonhierarchical" model of the Trinity and, most importantly, "its theology of universal salvation."

These are entertaining and thought-provoking books but shouldn't be confused with truth or being consistent with Biblical teachings.

Before moving on, I have a confession to make; I never returned the book I had "borrowed" from the radio station. I had every intention of doing so, but it became an integral part of my life—especially when I was traveling heavily for business. It made for great airplane reading! Yet, I still feel a little bad, because "thou shall not steal." But somehow I think Keith (and God) will forgive me. In fact, my keeping it may have been their intention all along.

Religious Services and Faith-Based Events

I am amazed at the number of Christians who declare, "I'm spiritual but not religious." When discussing this with a close friend, she told me that she had stopped going to church years ago. She then went on to say, "I'm a believer, but I don't need formal religion to have a relationship with God. I can experience Him during a walk in the woods or when watching a beautiful sunset." I remember another friend commenting on the same topic by saying, "I feel a lot closer to God when I'm out fishing early on a Sunday morning rather than going to church."

They're not alone. A survey by the Pew Research Center's Forum on Religion & Public Life conducted jointly with the

PBS television program *Religion & Ethics NewsWeekly*, finds that many of the country's 46 million unaffiliated adults are religious or spiritual in some way. Two-thirds of them say they believe in God (68%). More than half say they often feel a deep connection with nature and the earth (58%), while more than a third classify themselves as "spiritual" but not "religious" (37%). At the same time, people are fleeing organized religion in record numbers. According to a recent Gallup poll, fewer than 20% of Americans regularly attend church.

The Top Excuses for Not Attending Church Services

If you don't attend church services regularly, I suggest you seriously consider your reasons. I've heard all of the plausible reasons, but in my experience, they fall flat. In the following sections, I address a few of the more common excuses I've heard over the years.

» I'm too busy. I have too much going on.

During certain stages of our lives, our calendars become more cluttered, and our priorities change. Career, kids/sports, chores, shopping, recreational activities, and so on place greater demands on our time and energy. As our responsibilities grow and our priorities change, we need to be sure that God remains at the top of the list.

God must remain the top priority for two reasons: the here and now and the hereafter. By placing God first, we retain our intimate connection with the divine, which provides guidance and strength in all areas of our lives on earth. In the bigger scheme (eternity), placing God first is essential for ensuring the salvation of our immortal souls. What could be more important than that?

» Services are too boring and not anchored in today's challenges.

I often hear this from friends and family. Honestly, I've felt the same way at times. That many clergy don't receive training in public speaking is unfortunate. Their delivery runs the gamut from simply winging it to reading from something that equates to a script. Clergy should be able to connect with their audience, bringing scripture to life by tying it to everyday situations and challenges. If they don't have the requisite public speaking skills, they should enroll in a course or at least seek guidance through online educational resources.

If you feel that your church services are not fulfilling your needs or expectations, you have several options other than simply using it as an excuse for not attending. Here are a few suggestions:

- Shop around. Find a service and clergy you can relate to and vice versa. One word of caution: Shopping around is not about finding a message that's comfortable for you or a service that is entertaining. Rather, it's about our preferences. We all have distinct personalities that drive both the way we communicate and the way we like to be communicated to.
- Engage in the service. Participate by singing with other church members, reading along with the selections from scripture, taking notes during the sermon, and so on. The more active you are during a service, the more you will get out of it.
- Prepare yourself. We expect the clergy to be prepared, but we often overlook the preparation we need to do to reap the full benefit of a church service. Preparation includes participating in a Bible study group that meets regularly or meeting with clergy to improve your understanding of scriptures. By increasing your understanding of the scriptures, you are more likely to remain engaged during both the readings and the sermon.

» Too many people who go to church are hypocrites.

We all know people who claim to be devout, churchgoing Christians, but don't act that way outside of church. They're often the same people who check their religion at the office door Monday through Friday. We see their behavior in the office as being contradictory to their Christian faith; for example, the horrible, overbearing boss or the co-worker who takes all the credit for your ideas. We see hypocritical behavior on the roads and even in the church parking lot following services. Indeed, some are hypocrites. Most, though, are simply human. I, too, am guilty of un-Christian-like behavior, especially on the roads!

However, we shouldn't let the behavior of others deter us from attending services or interfering with our relationship with God. Even though we're Christians, we're still human and must live and operate in a world that challenges our faith. On days when we (or others) are not being our best selves, ask for forgiveness and forgive the hypocrite.

» Scandals among clergy members have driven me from the church.

Religious organizations are not immune from scandal. Churches in every denomination have experienced it in various forms—from priests or youth ministers molesting children to married ministers having affairs with members of the congregation to church leaders committing financial fraud.

Over the past decade, hundreds of people belonging to the Catholic Church have come forth with accounts of sexual abuse perpetrated by priests and covered up by Church hierarchy—from bishops to cardinals to archbishops. Some even allege that the cover up went as high up as the pope himself. Hundreds of millions of dollars have been paid out to settle lawsuits with many more suits pending. The Catholic Church has suffered a massive exodus as a result. I personally know of many who have left my own parish. Words cannot describe the damage that has

been done to the Church and the faithful. I completely understand why people would want to leave the Church.

Certainly, a full reckoning and a cleansing of all who committed the crimes as well as those involved in the cover-up is necessary. However, we need to keep in mind that the guilty clergy
members comprise a small part of the Church. Fewer than 7% of
the priests in the US were involved in the scandal. The other 93%
have served faithfully and honorably.

» I experience God best through nature.
As mentioned previously, many Christians believe they experience God through nature. No doubt that being in nature—whether on a mountain, near the ocean, or in the forest—can inspire intense spiritual feelings, but we shouldn't confuse creation for the
Creator. We are commanded to honor God, not God's creation.

To understand the foolishness of nature worship, read the following passage from The Wisdom of Solomon:

> For all men who were ignorant of God were fool-
> ish by nature; and they were unable from the good
> things that are seen to know him who exists, nor
> did they recognize the craftsman while paying
> heed to His works; but they supposed that either
> fire or wind or swift air, or the circle of the stars,
> or turbulent water, or the luminaries of heaven
> were the gods that rule the world.
>
> If through delight in the beauty of these things
> men assumed them to be gods, let them know
> how much better than these is their Lord, for the
> author of beauty created them.
>
> And if men were amazed at their power and
> working, let them perceive from them how much
> more powerful is He who formed them.

For from the greatness and beauty of created things comes a corresponding perception of their Creator.

Yet these men are little to be blamed, for perhaps they go astray while seeking God and desiring to find him.

For as they live among his works they keep searching, and they trust in what they see because the things that are seen are beautiful.

Yet again, not even they are to be excused; for if they had the power to know so much that they could investigate the world, how did they fail to find sooner the Lord of these things (Solomon 13:1-9 RSV).

The Top Reasons to Attend Weekly Church Service

If you are still on the fence regarding attending church on a weekly basis, consider the reasons for attending weekly church services, as presented in the following sections.

» It's a commandment.

The fourth commandment states, "Remember the Sabbath day, to keep it holy. Six days you shall labor, and do all your work, but the seventh day is a Sabbath to the Lord your God." For the Jewish faithful, the Sabbath begins with Friday sunset and ends at Saturday sunset. The early Christians celebrated the Sabbath on Sunday, given it was considered the first day of the week (consistent with the Gregorian calendar). In this case, the Sabbath extends from Saturday sunset to Sunday sunset.

Although the commandment does not explicitly state that we should observe the Sabbath by attending services, the intention is to refrain from unnecessary work and activities and focus on God. Attending church services is a surefire way to honor the commandment. Additional ways to keeping the Sabbath holy include prayer, reading scripture, and spending quality time with family and friends.

» Jesus and his family were observant Jews.

Christians often forget that first and foremost, Jesus was a Jew. Religion was an essential part of the Jewish faith. We know that the baby Jesus was presented at the Temple (to the elder) as was the custom. We know that Jesus was baptized at the Jordan River by John the Baptist. We know that Jesus attended synagogue and observed the Jewish holidays, most notably, Passover. He is the role model for Christians. If the Son of God thought religious observance was an important and integral part of life, why should we think it any less?

» The greatest Biblical figures were religious.

All of the major figures of the Old Testament (Abraham, Isaac, Jacob, Joseph, Moses, David, Solomon, Isaiah, etc.) worshipped God in various ways. Do you think God expects only His prophets and holy people to worship Him?

» We are a community of believers.

The New Testament contains numerous references to the Church representing the "Body of Christ." For instance, in Romans 12:5, Paul states, "So in Christ we, though many, form one body, and each member belongs to all the others." Members of the Body of Christ are the physical representation of Christ in this world.

Christ manifests His life to the world today through the one, holy Catholic and Apostolic Church. Note that the term "Catholic" is used here as an adjective deriving from the Greek (*katholikos*), meaning "universal." It is not a reference exclusively to the Roman Catholic Church but includes all denominations of the Christian faith.

Regardless of our denomination, as Christians, we are called to worship as a community of believers since we all share in the same heritage. In this way, we collectively honor and praise God. Additionally, we provide support to members of our community as well as those outside our community. Remember, Jesus sent his disciples out to preach the Good Word to all the nations.

How Would You Rate Yourself in Each Area of Faith Practices?

Prayer

1	2	3	4	5
Poor		Average		Excellent

Reading scripture and inspirational material

1	2	3	4	5
Poor		Average		Excellent

Attending religious services and faith-based events

1	2	3	4	5
Poor		Average		Excellent

Other (describe)

1	2	3	4	5
Poor		Average		Excellent

Tips for Strengthening Your Faith Practices

- Set goals for each practice category.
- Keep a log tracking how well you're doing in each category.
- Review your ratings at least once a week, and if you're not hitting your goals, identify the barriers—too many distractions, not enough time, other commitments, etc. Since you've committed to living your faith, make the appropriate adjustments in order to maintain your faith as your number one priority.

Faith Activation

Faith activation is the measure of the extent to which you *understand* and *apply* your:

- Unique talent
- Spiritual gifts
- Core values

Unique Talent

One thing we all have in common is that we share in the same heritage—we are children of God, created in His image. In this way we are the same.

But we also know that God has created us as unique human beings. Each of us is endowed with unique talents which come in many different forms.

Some possess great athletic abilities. Others have great intellectual capacity. Some are great at starting businesses, while others are better at running those businesses. I know gifted musicians, people who have the capacity to easily learn new languages, artists who seem born to draw, and mechanics who can fix just about anything. Everyone possesses varying degrees of different skills and abilities. What's important is how we choose to *apply* our natural gifts. For instance, you might have a strong command of words and language. How do you channel that? Perhaps as a journalist for a major newspaper, a novelist, a poet, or a screenwriter. You could start a blog based on your expertise on a particular subject. The same goes for any of our natural gifts—there are myriad possibilities. Our responsibility, as Christians, is to ask for God's guidance to discern the best way to develop and apply our unique talents and then put in the effort to do so.

Spiritual Gifts

Spiritual gifts are additional qualities or abilities bestowed upon us through the Holy Spirit. These gifts include service, teaching, prophecy, the ability to perform miracles, wisdom, knowledge, faith, mercy, leadership, and so on. In his letter to the Corinthians, Paul writes about these spiritual gifts:

> Brothers and sisters, I want you to know about the gifts of the Holy Spirit. You know that at one time you were unbelievers. You were somehow drawn away to worship statues of gods that couldn't even speak. So I want you to know that no one who is speaking with the help of God's Spirit says, "May Jesus be cursed." And without the help of the Holy Spirit no one can say, "Jesus is Lord."
>
> There are different kinds of gifts. But they are all given to believers by the same Spirit. There are different ways to serve. But they all come from the same Lord. There are different ways the Spirit works. But the same God is working in all these ways and in all people.
>
> The Holy Spirit is given to each of us in a special way. That is for the good of all. To some people, the Spirit gives a message of wisdom. To others, the same Spirit gives a message of knowledge.

To others the same Spirit gives faith. To others
that one Spirit gives gifts of healing. To others, he
gives the power to do miracles. To others, he gives
the ability to prophesy. To others, he gives the
ability to tell the spirits apart. To others, he gives
the ability to speak in different kinds of languages
they had not known before. And to still others, he
gives the ability to explain what was said in those
languages. All the gifts are produced by one and
the same Spirit. He gives gifts to each person, just
as he decides (1 Corinthians 12 NIRV).

In his Epistle to the Galatians, Paul admonishes (us) to "live
by the spirit and not by the flesh." He then describes the *"fruit
of the Spirit"* as love, joy, peace, patience, kindness, goodness,
faithfulness, gentleness, and self-control (Galatians 5:22 NIV).

We all possess the spiritual gifts and fruit of the Holy Spirit
but need to be more keenly aware of them and not withhold them
in service to others. St. Paul tells us in effect that God works
through us in different ways of His choosing. We can discern our
spiritual gifts through prayer as well as by seeking guidance from
clergy, family, and trusted friends. Our responsibility is to seek
ways to develop these gifts and use them to build the church, improve the communities in which we live, and ultimately glorify
God.

Core Values

Whether conscious of it or not, we all possess and are guided
by our core values—principles that guide our thoughts and behaviors, such as being honest, respecting others, doing the right
thing, working hard, and not giving up in the face of adversity.
Core values vary from person to person and can even change
in priority depending on circumstances. Though we shouldn't

impose our values on others, we should know our core values and have a firm grasp of how and when we should express them.

We should also be aware of and support the core values of our church and the other communities to which we belong, such as our workplace, sports leagues, and social groups (assuming those values align our own positive values and beliefs). Most churches have their own set of core values to help guide the congregation.

Unique talents

1	2	3	4	5
Poor		Average		Excellent

Spiritual gifts

1	2	3	4	5
Poor		Average		Excellent

Core values

1	2	3	4	5
Poor		Average		Excellent

THE 3RD POWER • 45

Tips for Strengthening Your Faith Activation

- Identify and list at least one unique talent, spiritual gift, and core value. For instance, unique talent: connecting people; spiritual gift: humility; core value: honesty.
- Make a point to look for opportunities to apply each talent, gift, and value at least once a day. For example, if you have a talent for connecting people, seek out someone in need of networking whether for career or relationships.

CHAPTER 2

Change Your Life by Changing Your Mind

To a large extent, Me Power depends on how we view circumstances—especially how we react when faced with challenging and sometimes life-changing situations.

Nate woke up in the hospital after a horrific car accident to everyone's worst nightmare: he was paraplegic at age 28.

An avid athlete and achievement-oriented person, Nate could not imagine how he could go on living without the use of his legs. He spent months lying in bed, utterly depressed. Then one day, he turned to God for help. "What should I do, God? How do I go on?" he asked.

He felt God answer him and knew that his life had been spared for a reason. "If you can't change your situation, change your mind," Nate heard God say. Nate started thinking positively. "I'm alive. I'm not going to waste my life. I'm going to make the best of it," he told himself.

Within months, Nate was strong and capable enough to get around in a wheelchair without assistance. Not long after that, he started competing in wheelchair sporting and bodybuilding events, which increased his enthusiasm for life even further. Today, Nate is married, has two children, and owns a successful business—all of which occurred since his accident. He's a living example of Me Power—trusting that God has equipped us with body, mind, and spirit to rise above our circumstances and achieve happiness and fulfillment.

The Power of Positive Thinking

Many of you are undoubtedly familiar with the phrase, "the power of positive thinking." It was coined back in the early 1950s by Dr. Norman Vincent Peale, who also authored a bestselling book of that title.

I had the great privilege of working for Dr. Peale's organization, The Center for Positive Thinking, back in 1995. I was tasked with adapting the principles of positive thinking to a new audience—businesspeople. During my research, I discovered that the original title of *The Power of Positive Thinking* was *The Power of Faith*. Dr. Peale's editor at the time argued that a book with the word "faith" in its title wouldn't sell very well. Furthermore, he said he noticed that Dr. Peale used the words "positive thinking" interchangeably with the word "faith." Dr. Peale agreed to the change.

Though Dr. Peale was a Methodist minister, he also was very interested in psychology and human behavior. He believed that we experience and communicate with the Divine through our mental faculties. Hence, our minds and faith are intertwined. I mention this because positive thinking has become common in everyday usage but means different things to different people. For the purposes of this chapter, I follow Dr. Peale's lead in using the phrases "positive thinking" and "faith" interchangeably.

Let's dig into what positive thinking means. Start by taking the Positive Thinking quiz.

What Do You Know about Positive Thinking?
Please mark each of the following statements True or False.

A. Negative people are born that way.

B. In most instances, what keeps people from fulfilling their potential are circumstances beyond their control.

C. Self-confidence is something that can be faked.

D. Saying that someone is a positive thinker is the same as saying that he or she is a Pollyanna.

E. Our beliefs shape our behaviors, which in turn shape our feelings.

F. Sometimes you have to ignore facts in order to be a positive thinker.

G. We cannot change the reality of most situations; we can control only our response to it.

H. Our self-expectations are usually not predictors of achievement.

I. Facts are more important than attitude.

J. If you don't make choices in your life, others will make them for you.

Now let's review.

Negative people are born that way.
False. Contrary to what many people believe, most negativity is *learned.*

Not long ago, I was having a discussion with a woman who was interested in participating in a positive thinking workshop. She was intrigued by the idea that positive thinking concepts could be brought into the workplace, yet skeptical about whether you can teach people to be positive. She presented the following line of reasoning: My husband is a natural-born positive thinker—always was, always will be. On the other hand, I have always been pessimistic—always was, always will be. Therefore, I'm inclined to think that either you have it or you don't, and if you don't, there's nothing you can do about it.

This woman views positive thinking as genetic. Just as some people are born with blue eyes and others with brown eyes, some are born optimists and others, pessimists. The fact, however, is that most of us are *born* positive thinkers. Although volumes of research support this fact, simple observation usually clears away all doubt. Infants generally have a positive attitude, assuming, of course, they are not sick, hungry, frustrated, or in need of a diaper change.

Many years ago, early in the morning, 5 a.m. to be exact, I was awakened by my then infant son, Andrew. I heard cooing noises and "senseless" chatter, as he was too young to form words. I arose, or rather stumbled, out of bed and subsequently into his room to see what was going on. I thought perhaps I could reason with him, talk some sense into him, to see if he'd be open to the idea of sleeping for a few more hours. The little guy greeted me with the biggest smile you've ever seen. If he could have talked at the time, I imagine he would have said something like "Good morning, Dad! Isn't it a terrific day? Let's play!"

Unfortunately, for many of us, this natural positive mindset is trained out of us. The average child hears the word "no" ten times more than the word "yes." Most of the time, the "no" is intended to prevent harm, but too often, it's delivered as a matter of convenience. Discouraging children from trying new things takes less time and effort than is required to encourage and teach.

In addition, the world and reality often pose significant challenges. As children pass through various stages of development, if they are not taught how to solve problems, communicate, build and maintain relationships, and so forth, failure and frustration can turn them from hopeful, confident dreamers into discouraged and disenchanted teenagers and ultimately adults.

In most cases, what keeps people from reaching their potential are circumstances beyond their control.
False. Actually, most barriers to reaching our potential are within our control.

We can group perceived barriers into two categories: *internal* and *external*. Internal barriers include fear, lack of confidence, feelings of inferiority, etc. Although time, effort, persistence, and patience are required to overcome internal barriers, we can control them to keep them from controlling us. That's good news because it means we don't have to (and shouldn't) rely on others to overcome them. We can shift our thinking to become more positive—and faith plays a key role in that, as explained later in this chapter.

External barriers are circumstances that people often perceive as being outside of their control. "It's the system holding me back!" we complain. "It's those crazy politicians working against me." "I've got too many responsibilities—children, a mortgage, an ill parent." "The company is downsizing."

When negative events occur, adopting a victim mentality is easy and far too common. The person with the victim mentality is always looking for excuses to explain away performance problems. Yes, many of us do suffer from the consequences of other people's decisions and actions, and some external events may be beyond our direct control. Nevertheless, we always can change our view of the circumstances and how we respond to them.

Self-confidence is something you can fake.
True. Yes, you can "Fake it till you make it!"

This answer always causes debate in the classroom when I'm teaching students at Fordham about the power of positive thinking. And the responses are usually split down the middle. "How can you fake something like self-confidence?" some will say. "If you're faking it, then it can't be self-confidence!" That argument contains some truth, but you really can fake self-confidence, for a little while anyway.

One of the greatest fears known to human beings is public speaking. Our hearts race, palms sweat, knees tremble. And yet, with a little training and practice, many people can get on stage and deliver a wonderful performance—in spite of their anxiety.

However, you can't fake anything forever—nor should you try. I am not suggesting that you become insincere or phony. Rather this technique, known as "act-as-if," has roots in behavioral psychology. Studies have shown that if you put on a smile, your brain responds to the movement of your facial muscles, and you actually feel happier. So even if you don't feel joyful, serene, or confident, try acting that way for a while and see if it helps. Chances are it will.

Saying someone is a positive thinker is the same as saying the person is a Pollyanna.
False. Positive thinking does not equate with being naïve.

In Pollyanna's defense, her bad rap is undeserved and unfair. Unfortunately, over the years, and due to our unfamiliarity with the original story, the expression "Pollyanna" has taken on a negative connotation. But the character Pollyanna, from the 1913 novel of the same title written by Eleanor H. Porter, was anything but a stumbling, hapless, naïve girl. On the contrary, she was a positive thinker. Orphaned at eleven years of age and forced to live with her mean-spirited Aunt Polly, Pollyanna had learned from her father, a minister, to always try to find the good in every situation. Although life dealt her a difficult hand, she managed to maintain an even disposition and hope-filled outlook on life. As a result, she was able to bring about incredible changes in the most negative people—particularly her aunt.

Based on our misplaced perceptions, Pollyanna has come to be seen as a naïve, unrealistic child. And a positive thinker is definitely not that. The distinguishing characteristic of a positive thinker is that she makes the best out of challenging situations. Equipped with a strong faith in God, positive thinkers are reality-based and willing to tackle problems head-on—with a positive attitude.

Our beliefs shape our behaviors, which in turn shape our feelings.
False. Our beliefs shape our feelings, which in turn shape our behaviors.

At first glance, the order of this statement looks logical. But it is actually slightly out of order. Our beliefs, which are responsible for our thoughts, shape our feelings, which in turn shape our behaviors. Feelings and behaviors are often confused because they appear to pose a "chicken and egg" dilemma. Which comes first, the feeling or the behavior? Definitely our feelings. We'll explore this concept further later in this chapter.

Sometimes you have to ignore the facts to be a positive thinker.
True. But only with clarification.

This statement is controversial and never fails to get people's attention. The word that evokes such strong reactions is "ignore." I don't mean to suggest that we should not be aware of and acknowledge the facts. What I mean is that before we abandon an idea or a course of action because of a certain set of facts, we ought to consider suspending or temporarily ignoring the facts, so we can remain open to new sets of facts.

I'm a huge Starbucks fan. In his book *Pour Your Heart Into It*, Starbucks' Chairman and CEO Howard Schulz talks about all the naysayers he encountered when trying to grow his coffee business. They provided plenty of reasons, based on facts, not to proceed with his ideas. He writes:

> We had no lock on the world's supply of fine coffee, no patent on the dark roast. . . . I heard all the arguments about why coffee could never be a growth industry. It was the second most widely traded commodity in the world, after oil. Consumption of coffee had been falling in America since the mid-60s.

Many people also told him that people would not pay for premium coffee. Of course, he proved them wrong. Starbucks now has more than 24,000 stores in over 70 countries and opens hundreds more each year. Howard Schulz acted *despite* the facts and the conclusions most people drew from the facts.

The key here is to identify the facts, acknowledge them, and then creatively discover ways to move forward. Too many of us let the facts bury us. Instead of using them to our advantage, we transform them into barriers and ultimately into excuses for not taking a particular course of action.

Roger Bannister was the first human being in recorded history to run a four-minute mile. Until 1954, no one had been able to achieve that feat. The experts at the time (physiologists, medical doctors, etc.) argued that it was humanly impossible. They presented facts suggesting that the human anatomy simply was not designed for it. Roger was not convinced—and he proved them wrong.

During the next 18 months, 24 more runners broke the four-minute mark. Incredible! What happened? Did they try some new steroid, vitamin, or sneaker? Did they train harder? No, none of the above. They simply believed it was possible because a new set of facts had been introduced by Bannister, who had consciously decided to push "the facts" aside.

We cannot change the reality of most situations; we can control only our responses to it.
True. Most of what happens to us is outside of our control, but we have complete control over our *responses* to situations.

All too often, we get caught-up in trying to change events that are beyond our control, such as a natural disaster, company layoffs, or even someone falling out of love. It's all a waste of time and energy. We cannot go back and undo the past, and we often do not have direct influence over the decisions and actions of others. However, we definitely do have a choice in how we react.

We can choose to be bitter, angry, resentful, or depressed, or we can choose to be positive, to forgive, let go, and take action to make our lives better going forward.

Our self-expectations are usually not a predictor of achievement.
False. Self-expectations are very much a predictor of future success.

As the old saying goes, "Expect the best and get the best. Expect the worst and get the worst." Like a magnet, our positive expectations draw the best toward us. Negative expectations repel the best and draw the worst to us. When we expect success, we fundamentally change our inner selves. Our attitude becomes hopeful and confident. This positive disposition is conveyed through our body language and through what we say and how we say it. Our behavior, in turn, affects people around us in positive ways.

Facts are more important than attitude.
False. As we discussed in number six, our view of the facts is much more important than the facts themselves.

In essence, if you think you can overcome an obstacle, chances are much higher that you can. If you start seeing a situation as impossible, you'll never find a way to make it better.

If you don't make choices in your life, others will make them for you.
True. When we fail to make a decision, we often put ourselves at the mercy of others.

Life is full of choices. Positive thinking enables us to make decisions. Negative thinking makes us indecisive. Fear, worry, confusion, and lack of confidence paralyze us. Positive thinking empowers us by giving us hope in a better world and faith in ourselves—thanks to God.

Examples

Here are just a few examples of how the power of positive thinking can have an impact on people everywhere, every day.

Somewhere . . .
A high school student is being told for the first time that he has the potential to do more than he thought possible.

Somewhere else . . .
A high school student is being told again he is not smart enough to get into college or make something of his life, and thus he drops out of high school.

Somewhere . . .
An actress has taken the stage for the first time.

Somewhere else . . .
An actress has attended her last audition, deciding that her dream of making it on Broadway is over. She returns to her office job.

Somewhere . . .
Someone has written the next great American novel.

Somewhere else . . .
A manuscript sits unsent, its owner afraid of rejection.

Somewhere . . .
Someone at a sewing machine just designed the next dress fawned over at the Oscars.

Somewhere else . . .
A dress hangs in a closet, never seen, because the designer didn't think it was worthy of showing to anyone.

Somewhere . . .

The owners of a new restaurant just pinned their first dollar to the wall to the cheers of patrons and wait staff.

Somewhere else . . .
A fabulous cook relinquished his dream to open a new restaurant, convinced that the competition among restaurateurs made the venture too risky. Doors never opened, cuisine was never tasted, another dream went unfulfilled.

Changing How You Think

One evening, an aged American Indian of the Chippewa tribe told his grandson a story. "My son," he said, "There is a battle between two wolves inside us all. One wolf is evil. It is anger, envy, jealousy, sorrow, regret, greed, arrogance, self-pity, guilt, resentment, inferiority, lies, false pride, superiority, and ego. The other wolf is good. It is joy, peace, love, hope, serenity, humility, kindness, benevolence, empathy, generosity, truth, compassion, and faith."

The grandson thought about it for a minute and then asked his grandfather, "Which wolf wins?"

The old man replied, "The one you feed."

Reorienting how we think in order to make better decisions begins with an understanding of how the mind works—an understanding of how we can feed the "good wolf" while starving the "bad wolf."

Joanna is a mid-level manager at a large bank. She is always bubbling with new ideas. Yet she has noticed that her boss, Eileen, never seems to pay attention to her.

Just today, Joanna stopped by Eileen's desk. "I've come up with a great way for us to reduce costs, Eileen," she spouted excitedly as her boss glanced up from her computer. "It has to do with yield. . . ." But she paused because she could see that Eileen's eyes were already glazing over.

"It doesn't matter," Joanna thought to herself as she stormed away. "I don't matter. No one pays attention to me. I should stop trying."

The reason why Joanna acted the way she did was that she made negative assumptions about the situation. This affected her *thoughts* (what she was telling herself), evoking a strong emotional *feeling* (anger), causing her to take *action* (storm out of the room). Essentially, she made a choice to follow a negative course leading to an undesirable outcome.

Cognitive-behavioral psychologists have identified a chain reaction referred to as BTFA: Beliefs—Thoughts—Feelings—Actions. What we believe about a situation ("I don't matter.") determines our thoughts ("No one pays attention to me."). Our thoughts, in turn, impact our feelings (worthlessness, hurt, frustration), which influence our actions ("I should just stop trying.")

How the Mind Works

In the case of Joanna, if she could simply change her belief to a positive one ("I *do* matter."), this would impact her thoughts ("I need to figure out a way to communicate my ideas more effectively."), which in turn would alter her feelings (self-empowerment, motivation to find a solution), and, therefore, her actions (e.g., setting up a meeting to present her ideas when Eileen is able to fully pay attention, researching her ideas so that she has data to back them up, getting the buy-in of key colleagues before the meeting, and so on).

The implications of this simple model are profound. If you want to feed the good wolf—that is, feel happy and be as effective

THE 3RD POWER • 59

and efficient as possible—start by *believing* that you are a worthwhile, gifted human being who can achieve whatever you set your mind to. Then make a deliberate effort to talk to yourself in a positive manner. As soon as you begin to focus on seeing the good side of situations and people, you will feel better about yourself and the world, and your actions will have more positive outcomes.

Changing our thoughts from negative to positive also requires that we monitor our self-talk and address self-limiting beliefs, replacing them with self-empowering beliefs.

Let's take a look at both.

Negative Self-Talk

Changing our thoughts from negative to positive requires that we closely examine our self-talk. The fact is, we all talk to ourselves all day long. If you are thinking, you are talking to yourself and seeing flashes of images as well. Self-talk is what we tell ourselves under certain circumstances. Some people refer to it as our inner dialogue. It's like having a stereo system in your head.

Our typical responses are burned into our minds. When faced with various situations, we automatically hit the "play" button, and the same message plays, time and again.

Your boss is not listening to you, so you fast forward to the "my boss is a jerk" track.

Management is restructuring again, so you start playing, "Those morons have no idea what they're doing."

By listening to our self-talk, we discover whether our automatic responses—especially to tough, challenging situations—are rational and constructive or irrational and destructive. How you talk to yourself all day long has a major impact on how you feel and perform. Think of something going on right now in your life that happens to be particularly challenging: an argument with your partner or teenager, a task you don't want to perform on the job, your car breaking down. What "song" do you hear being played in your mind?

Here are some examples of self-sabotaging, negative self-talk:

- As usual, the situation is all fouled up.
- I can't catch a break.
- This is killing me. I can't take it anymore.
- This is do or die. I'm going to choke.
- Here goes nothing.
- I'm not a writer. Why do I have to prepare this report?
- He's a louse. I can't stand him.
- Oh yeah, like they really care about us.
- They've never bought from us before. I don't know why they will now.
- Every time I call them, I get the runaround.
- If this works, it will be a miracle.
- I'm no good at this.
- I'm such a jerk. How could I make a mistake like that?

"When the mind talks, the body listens. We literally talk ourselves into and out of every victory or defeat in the game of life," says Dr. Denis Waitley, a scientist who has studied human performance for over 20 years.

Negative self-talk usually centers on lacking a resource, such as time, money, or information; dwells on a past loss or the possibility of a future loss ("here we go again, the same lousy outcome as last time I tried this..."); or focuses on a personal shortcoming ("I don't have the proper background and experience..."), while ignoring personal strengths. Every type of negative self-talk is very likely to set you up for failure. What the mind dwells upon, the body acts upon.

As you go through the day, monitor your self-talk. Whenever you catch yourself saying something negative about yourself, the situation you are in, or about other people, see if you can find a positive angle to focus on. As you know, you can choose to view the glass of life as half empty or half full. Both viewpoints are true and equally valid, but one view helps you to think creatively and get what you want, while the other limits your options, thereby working against you.

Self-Limiting Beliefs

Just as negative self-talk limits our ability to achieve what we want in life, so do self-limiting beliefs (SLBs). Here are a few examples of SLBs:

- People must treat me fairly.
- I should have little discomfort in life.
- People must find me likable.
- It's awful when I make a mistake.
- I must be the best at everything or I'm no good.
- People who treat me badly deserve to be punished.
- I deserve to get what I want when I want it.
- I cannot control how I feel.

Now let's take a closer look at each one of these universal SLBs, including some sample phrases associated with each, and show how they affect performance.

People must treat me fairly.

"How can they do that to me after all I've done for them?"

"My kids just don't appreciate all the help I've given them!"

"After 20 years of marriage as a loyal, dedicated wife, he up and leaves me."

"I worked so hard preparing a nice meal, how dare they not like it!"

"I spend hours each week helping others; now when I need a hand there's no one there to help."

Nothing is wrong with expecting fair treatment in exchange for giving fair treatment to others. But what happens if we hold this SLB in absolute terms and someone does not treat us fairly? We are likely to be disappointed, perhaps vindictive. Instead, we ought to offer fair treatment regardless of how others treat us. We're better off accepting that our parents were right, and life isn't fair. Not only that, but none of us is the absolute moral authority, and sometimes our limited perceptions or misunderstanding of the word "fairness" are what caused the problem in the first place.

I should have little discomfort in life.

"Here we go again, another re-organization. Why do they have to do that to me?"

"I can't believe they want me to serve as a volunteer on yet another committee!"

"Like I really need the aggravation of waiting in this long line right now!"

"Why can't the utility company get back to me right away? They're taking forever to restore power."

"What a hassle to have to write all these reports. They don't read half of them anyway!"

This SLB is very self-centered. Where is it written that life should be easy and we should be comfortable? Instead of complaining and running away from discomfort, we need to shift our perception of discomfort. Here are a few ways to think about discomfort more positively:

- Approach discomfort as an opportunity. Think about all the inventions that have come about as solutions to problems and ways to ease daily burdens.
- Approach discomfort as a challenge. What can you do (other than complain) to eliminate or minimize the source of your discomfort?

- Think outside of yourself. Try instead to focus on the other people in your life and their needs.

People must find me likable.

"What did I do to cause Sue to dislike me so much?"

"I'm going to compliment Keith on his golf game, even though I don't think it's great."

"Nobody likes me. That's why I never get any good opportunities around here."

"I couldn't stand it if Jane were mad at me!"

Often, we make poor life decisions because we fear being rejected or having people disapprove of us. For some of us, the need to be accepted and to fit in is so strong that we fail to be honest with other people about their actions. "If I tell Keith what I really think of his idea, he'll be upset with me for a long time. I have to work with him every day—I couldn't handle it."

Wanting to be liked by others is okay. In fact, according to the famous psychologist Abraham Maslow, it is one of the strongest needs that human beings experience. But insisting that people "must" find us likeable negatively impacts our conduct.

A better, more constructive way to deal with our need to be liked is to focus on self-respect. We can't make people like us. What we can do is work on ourselves. We can think, feel, and act more securely and confidently, knowing that others are attracted to these traits. We also can concentrate on liking others versus being liked by others. So instead of being absorbed by our own needs, we think about the needs of others in a sincere way, without any expectation of personal gain.

I remember talking to my cousin Phil one afternoon on this subject. As he often does, he had a useful perspective that has stuck with me to this day. He said, "You know, Scott, people try to win the approval of others by trying to be interesting. They talk about themselves most of the time. They never ask questions of the other person, and when the other person speaks they don't listen. Instead of trying to be interesting, we should try harder to be interested in the other person." When we are genuinely interested in others, people respond positively.

It's awful when I make a mistake.
"I'm no good; I can't get anything right!"
    "What an idiot! I can't believe I just did that."
    "I don't deserve a second chance."
    "I'll never get the promotion now."
    "It's just way too risky. Better not try."
This is very similar to the previous SLB, but it can cause even more damage. As a consultant, I have had the opportunity to work and associate with some exceptionally bright people over the years, and I am amazed at the number of them whose happiness depends on how well they perform. Anything less than perfect is failure—whether at school, at work, or in their personal lives.

This feeling is self-imposed. Unlike feeling like a bad person if you make a mistake, the source of feeling unworthy if you aren't perfect is inherent competitiveness. For such people, their fiercest competitors are themselves! They are harder on themselves than they are on others.

At the Fordham business school where I teach, I have had many talented students who are incredibly hard on themselves. Once I received a call from a bright young man asking what he could do to bring his grade up from an "A−" to an "A."

"I just gotta have an A, professor," he said. "If I don't, my GPA will drop below a 4.0. I couldn't live with myself if that happened."

Some of my students mentally and physically abuse themselves if they fall short of the goal. We live in an achievement-oriented society in which so many of us view ourselves as failures if we don't measure up 100% of the time.

At school, at home, and in the workplace, this SLB has a double negative impact on performance. First of all, the perfectionist takes much more time and requires more resources to complete certain tasks than necessary. Such people can't follow the "80/20 Rule" and decide when it's best to just quickly knock a few items off the to-do list. They can become mired in minor tasks and totally overwhelmed. Yet, the corresponding benefits of seeking perfection are not commensurate with the effort they invested. In short, they often end up wasting time. Second, because we all are fallible human beings, perfection is actually unattainable. Even so, when the perfectionist fails to achieve the unachievable, she often ends up suffering from depression and anxiety, burning out, or even experiencing a total breakdown. The result can be costly in terms of both treatment and lost opportunity.

I must be the best at everything or I'm no good.
"If I don't get the top grade forget it, I'm a failure."

"Things had better go smoothly because if they don't, I'll look really bad."

"I better not make a move just yet—I may not have all the information."

"They have to pick my idea or I'm a miserable failure."

No one can possibly be the best at everything. It's important to know what your talents are as well as your limitations. Focus on your strengths and apply yourself to the development of your God-given capabilities. Never mind what others may think of you—they have their own insecurities.

People who treat me badly deserve to be punished.
"It's your fault that this is happening."

"John will pay for that if it's the last thing I do."

"She's finally going to get what's coming to her."

"That's the last time I do anything for Mary."

Calculating the costs associated with "getting even" with people who have done us wrong is difficult. Few of us care to admit that we spend time and energy in this way, yet many of us are prone to this SLB. We assign ourselves the role of judge and jury, creating a punishment we feel fits the crime. This vengefulness has a negative impact because it converts positive energy that could be used in productive ways into negative energy that has no benefits.

We may exact punishment in a number of ways: by undermining another's efforts, criticizing the offender's ideas, gossiping or posting to social media with the intention of hurting or destroying the other person, and so forth. In addition to the damage caused to one's soul, such actions have a direct negative impact on the perpetrator's bottom line. A report in the the *Wall Street Journal* cited a survey conducted by the University of North Carolina business school. This study found that as a result of incivility, 22% of respondents had deliberately decreased their work output, and 52% lost time at work worrying.

A few years back, a well-known NFL player admitted that while working on an automobile assembly line, he placed extra hardware (e.g., nuts, bolts, washers) inside the door frame so that it would rattle like crazy when the car was driven. He did this because he felt that he had been wronged by the automaker and so he "was getting back at them."

A healthier mindset in dealing with injustice and incivility is to realize that most individuals are basically good people. But even basically good people sometimes do bad things—and most of the time it is unintentional.

There's a great line in the classic movie *The Wizard of Oz*. Towards the end, Dorothy, feeling cheated by the Wizard, chastises him saying, "You're a very bad man!"

He replies, "Oh no, my dear, I'm just a bad Wizard."

The implication is that although some of his actions in the role of Wizard produced undesirable results, he was fundamentally a good person.

Obsessing about the perceived wrongs suffered at the hands of others or getting even with people is harmful to us and counterproductive overall. The energy we expend could be put to positive use. I hold the conviction that we should never use negative energy to deal with negative situations. If anything, we should either redirect the energy in more useful ways or meet the negative energy with positive energy.

Negative energy crumbles under the enormous power of positive energy. Generating and directing positive energy certainly takes time, effort, and fortitude, but eventually you produce better results and feel better about yourself and the world around you.

In the course of my professional life, I have negotiated many deals and contracts. In one case, a dispute arose regarding the interpretation of certain language in the contract. I felt I was being unfairly treated. My first reaction was to hire a lawyer and go after the company. After I thought about it, though, I realized I would spend far too much time and energy on something that, in the grand scheme of things, was not all that important to me. I let it go and redirected my efforts into growing my business.

The sweet feelings of revenge are brief, leaving a bitter aftertaste as we reflect on our return on investment. Engaging in such hurtful behaviors will catch up to us sooner or later. As tempting as it might be, and as justified as you may feel, stay away from vindictiveness—forgive.

I deserve to get what I want when I want it.
"Come on let's go. I don't have all day, you know!"

"If you can't make up your mind by tomorrow, you can just forget it!"

"Never mind what Kathryn wants. I need you to take care of this now!"

"Tell your friends they'll have to wait. This is too important to me."

This SLB reminds me of a song from a Broadway musical. Although I don't remember the name of the musical, I do recall the lyrics, which go like this: "I want what I want when I want it, and I want it NOW!"

This SLB is based on a feeling of self-importance. It drives impatient, demanding behavior, throwing an individual's personal life or the organization they work for into turmoil. The feeling that "the world revolves around me" may come from different sources. People who have had everything handed to them on a silver platter, or who have attained a certain status in life, are likely to adopt this attitude.

If you have this SLB and don't learn how to deal with it, you risk driving good people away. How many times have you heard from a friend or coworker (or spouse or child) something like, "No matter how hard I try, I can't seem to please you"? If you have, that's not a good sign. Take note. Individuals with this ingrained attitude are not likely to change overnight. It requires deepening one's self-awareness and understanding and developing a greater tolerance of others. You will need to remind yourself constantly that you are not the center of the universe. People have other goals and priorities that don't always fit into your timetable.

I cannot control how I feel.
"That's just the way I am. There's nothing I can do about it."
"Look, I've always been like this. You'll have to get used to it."
"Who wouldn't react this way?"
"I'm sorry that I hollered at you, but I can't help it."

I call this SLB "the big excuse." It covers for a lot of inappropriate behavior, including yelling, ranting and raving, name-calling, and other unprofessional conduct. I know people who have been plagued with this problem, and it has hurt them professionally, derailing otherwise promising careers.

I once coached a businessman who was upset with himself because he lost control of his temper—often. He realized that if it happened one more time, he'd be fired as he already had been warned on a number of occasions.

"I'm afraid this is it for me," he told me. "You see, Scott, I've been like this all my life. I want to change, but I can't. It's just the way I am."

What a sad statement. It is filled with self-defeating language. It suggests that we, as people, are fundamentally unchangeable.

The truth is that, until forced, most people won't do anything about their counterproductive behaviors because change takes hard work, self-evaluation, and honesty. Most people would rather take the easy way out and just blame their past personal history ("It was the way I was brought up."), DNA ("I'm Italian; we're all emotional."), or some significant event in life ("I was teased as a child."). Quite often, they are enabled by others. A colleague, mother, husband, or friend will say, "Oh, don't mind Pete, that's just the way he is. Don't take it personally."

The first step toward overcoming this SLB is to realize that regardless of how ingrained you might think a bad habit is, you can change it. People do it all the time. They stop hitting, yelling, drinking, gambling, or doing any number of undesirable activities. Yes, it may require tremendous effort, but it is possible and worthwhile. You don't want to wait until your job, health, an important relationship, or all three are at risk.

According to psychologist Albert Ellis, all self-limiting beliefs can be reduced to one of the three core irrationalities:

- An impulse to self-denigration
- Intolerance or frustration
- Blaming and condemning others

High-performing individuals are in step with reality. They do not blow things out of proportion or read too much into situations. They accept the fact that difficult people and unpleasant situations come with the territory. They also understand that they—and all of us—are imperfect. They put their inevitable mistakes and failures into perspective, learn from them, and move forward in pursuit of their goals.

We all, to some degree, have self-limiting beliefs that get in the way of stellar performance. Understanding them and their impact on our behavior is an important first step in dealing with them. But can we overcome them, and if so how?

Truth in Thinking

Answer the following six questions to achieve truth in thinking:

A. What is the event that has triggered your upset?
B. What are you telling yourself about the event? (What's your self-talk?)
C. Is what you're telling yourself in line with the world as it truly is or how you wish it (or insist it) to be? (Check your self-talk against the list of self-limiting beliefs.)
D. What is a more realistic, rational, constructive way of viewing the event?
E. How can viewing the event in a more realistic, rational, constructive way benefit you and any others involved?
F. How can you change your original self-talk to self-talk that reflects your new perspective on the event?

Let's look at an example:

We've all experienced waiting at an airport or, even worse, on board an aircraft for a long-delayed flight. It's frustrating and annoying. Our self-talk might sound something like this: "Why does this always have to happen to me? I can't believe it. I'll never make the meeting now. Get me out of here. Stupid airlines are always screwing up." We sit and stew, lashing out at anybody who crosses our path.

Is our reaction rational? Which self-limiting beliefs are at work here? Some of us believe that things should always go smoothly and are intolerant when things don't. Others like to play the blame game. Others sink immediately into self-criticism.

A better way to view this event is to see the positive aspects of the situation. The delay may be due to bad weather or a mechanical failure, which means that the flight is being held up for our own safety. Would we rather die in a plane crash? I'm guessing the answer is no.

Viewing the delay in this way saves us undo aggravation and misery. We can change our self-talk to reflect a more positive mindset: "I'd rather be safe than sorry. I'll just call ahead and let everyone know that I'll be delayed. Joanne can cover for me anyway if they have to start without me. I'm going to sit back, relax, and catch up on my reading. There's nothing I can do about it anyway."

People I coach have been amazed at the power and effectiveness of this simple process. It's powerful because it helps bring subconscious irrational, self-limiting beliefs to a conscious level, where we can challenge them and then replace them with more productive thoughts.

Too frequently, we pay attention only to our resulting behaviors, without examining the subconscious beliefs that are responsible for them. As a result, we behave in ways that even we can't explain. But when we take a moment to notice and question our self-limiting beliefs, we are able to draw links to negative behaviors. Then by applying truth-in-thinking in stressful or upsetting situations, we can begin to minimize these behaviors.

I've found that most people won't admit, at least in public, that they possess one or more of the self-limiting beliefs. But even the most seasoned managers have told me, privately, how much they really do hold some SLBs close, and how this concept has helped them overcome negativity in their work and personal lives.

If you diligently and regularly apply this habit of turning inward to your own thoughts, beliefs, and reactions during tough situations, over time you will develop an awareness of certain recurring self-limiting beliefs. This will help you get your emotions under control quickly. It will also improve your relationships, and our success in life is ultimately dependent upon the commitment, loyalty, and support of those around us.

CHAPTER 3

The Platinum Standard—Your Personal GPS

My personal conviction is that, by and large, people want to be good. They want to "do the right thing," and they have a broad intuitive sense of what that means. But in today's world—with corporations, the government, the church, and traditional family structure all collapsing—people have few places to turn for trusted advice in making difficult decisions or forming their own ethical principles. Where are we supposed to look for inspiration and moral guidance? Once again, the answer lies within. As I've mentioned before, hidden in every person is some of the Divine. It is this spirit that makes us do the right thing at the right time. I refer to this as the "Platinum Standard."

The Platinum Standard

Many people have strayed from their core beliefs, either compromising them or lowering their standards. Some have abandoned their values completely, adopting an "everybody does it" mentality. A Platinum Standard is a personal ethical framework that serves as a compass, guiding us to think and act with integrity when the moral landscape grows fuzzy.

Why do I call it the Platinum Standard? In Washington D.C., within the walls of the National Bureau of Standards, is a one-meter length of platinum, which exists as the most perfect measure of a meter. If any doubt arises regarding the length of a meter, one can reference the platinum standard to determine the true measure. It is made of platinum because that material does not break down. It does not rust, corrode, expand, or shrink. It is virtually unchangeable.

The Platinum Standard I present in this chapter is based on an interwoven set of morals, principles, values, and beliefs that evolve throughout our lives. At its core, it is a personal standard of integrity—a commitment to acting with honesty, openness, and fairness. It serves as an anchor, firmly grounding us before as well as during our daily activities. For some, it is founded on religious principles (e.g., the Ten Commandments or the Golden Rule). For others, it is based on universal humanistic principles (treat people fairly, honestly, courteously, etc.). Both draw from the inner divinity that God has placed in all of us.

Clarifying what our Platinum Standard is and maintaining our awareness of it will guide our actions even when faced with the most challenging moral and ethical dilemmas.

"Lie or Lose Your Job"

Integrity has been a subject close to my heart for my entire life. But it came to the forefront when I was in my early 30s. An ethical dilemma required me to act with moral courage and make my personal commitment to living with integrity explicit.

I was working at a medium-sized company, and my prospects there seemed to be excellent. I was in charge of my own project, which was going well. I enjoyed the freedom and made twice the effort to surpass expectations.

Then one day, the president called me into his office. "Scott," he said, "as you know we're scheduled to have a board meeting next week. I'd like you to call the chairman and tell him that the meeting has been cancelled."

"Why was the meeting cancelled?" I asked.

"Well actually, it wasn't. But I don't want the chairman to be there. We're going to be making some critical strategic decisions about how to move our company forward, and the chairman will fight them. He's living in the twentieth century.

"He just doesn't understand how the business world has evolved in the past decade due to globalization and technology. He could do serious damage to our plans. As you know, if we don't make some major changes, we could be in trouble financially. So I need you to tell him that the meeting is off."

I sat uncomfortably in my chair, turning deep shades of purple, rubbing my sweaty palms together. Lying to the chairman of the board seemed obviously wrong to me, and I was shocked that the president would even ask me to do such a thing. On the other hand, if the chairman's opinions might put the company in jeopardy, then perhaps I should do as the president directed. I also feared retribution by the president if I didn't act on his request.

I gave no response, which I believe now the president took as a sign of agreement to lie on his behalf. But I did not make the call. It just didn't feel right.

A week later, I dressed in my best suit and nervously entered the conference room for our board meeting. The president was there, as were the CEO and a dozen other key players, but the chairman was not. I wondered if by some miracle he had been unable to attend or if the president had made the call himself. We stood around the bagels and coffee, chatting for a few minutes, my heart pounding wildly. Then the chairman entered the room and confidently took his seat. The president shot me a look that said, "Ventrella, you're dead meat."

A few days later, the CEO called me into his office. I had a feeling he didn't have good news. He gave me a sincerely apologetic look and then told me that since the company was going through a tough time, I would no longer be able to operate my own project independently.

He was going to put me under the direct supervision of the president. I blanched. Not only would I be losing my autonomy, but also I would be working daily for a person whom I did not respect.

Right there, I had to make a choice: stay on in this new and uncomfortable position or resign. Given what had happened with the board meeting, I knew that the president was getting his payback. I thought about mentioning his request that I lie to the chairman, but I decided not to say anything. Best to just leave it alone. It took genuine moral courage for me to give my answer because I needed the money. But in my heart, I knew that this work situation would not allow me to operate in line with my values. I expressed my appreciation for having had the opportunity to be a part of his team, and then I let the CEO know that he was going to have to accept my resignation.

I went home that night and told my wife, the mother of our toddler and newborn baby, that I had stayed true to my values and as a result was out of a job. She supported me whole-heartedly, though we both worried about how we would make it through financially. We agreed just to have faith that everything would work out for us.

In the coming weeks, I scraped together enough consulting work to pay the mortgage, and we cut back on expenses. Six months later, I got a surprise call from the CEO of the company. He wanted me to come into the office to meet with him immediately.

When I got there, he apologized profusely for having doubted me. He told me that he had received several serious complaints about the president's behavior in the past months. He knew now that the president had demanded that I behave unethically and that I had refused. He admired me greatly for acting with integrity. He asked me to come back at a higher salary and in a more senior position. I accepted.

My integrity had paid off—this time, at least. But I understood that I was lucky. The world doesn't always play fair. I realized then the complexity of making ethical decisions, the deep motivators that lead people to behave in opposition to their values, and the stress that people can suffer as a result. I vowed to stay true to my morals and beliefs going forward in my life no matter what.

One of my favorite definitions of integrity is this: "Integrity is what we do when no one is watching."

J.P. Hayes wasn't playing golf just for fun; he was playing for a full-time spot on the 2009 PGA Tour. On the 12th hole of his first round, Hayes' caddie reached into his bag and tossed Hayes a ball. Hayes made two shots with the ball before realizing that it was a prototype not approved for use in competition. Although no one would have known about his mistake if Hayes had pocketed the ball and continued to play out the tournament, he realized that he had unintentionally broken the rules. Later that day, he called an official and disqualified himself from the tournament. Hayes admitted later that the accident was "extremely disappointing," but added that anyone else in his situation "would have done the same thing."

I wish I could say that were the case. The truth is many athletes—and people in general—would not have made the same choice as Hayes, who blew the whistle on himself. For example, track star Marion Jones admitted to using steroids to earn her five medals in the 2000 Sydney Olympics only after several years of angry denials. Hayes stands out from the crowd because he knew his ethical standards, and he acted in accordance with them immediately in spite of the significant consequences. Hayes offers a living example of what operating with integrity entails.

The word "integrity" is derived from the Latin word integer, meaning "whole." Living with integrity gives us the inner sense of wholeness that comes from acting conscientiously. It's not merely a moral or principled idea or position; it requires action in accordance with one's conscience. We demonstrate integrity each time we:

- Use consistent and appropriate criteria to measure our own performance.
- Rely on our ethics, morals, and principles to guide our thoughts and actions.
- Avoid undermining or criticizing others behind their backs.
- Admit to our weaknesses and areas that need improvement.
- Acknowledge others' efforts and give them credit for their contributions.
- Strive to create "win-win" outcomes with others.
- Do what is right, even though easier, more expedient options are available.

How do we know when we are acting with integrity? Philosophers have developed a wide variety of theories to describe and guide moral and ethical human behavior. Eighteenth century philosopher Immanuel Kant presented what I think is the most sensible and practical opinion. He proposed two rules for judging our behavior:

A. Reversibility: What if someone did to you what you are about to do to him? Would you find that acceptable? This is a version of the Golden Rule.
B. Universality: What if whatever action you're about to take established a rule that permitted everyone in the world to do it? What would you do then?

Asking these two simple questions in tricky situations can help to guide your thoughts and actions.

Gauging Your Integrity Standards

A great way to evaluate your integrity standards is to perform the interactive Four Corners exercise. I have used this exercise dozens of times in my courses at Fordham and Fairfield Universities and in corporate and managerial ethics seminars. It never fails to generate a great deal of excitement and critical questioning of the meaning of integrity. This exercise will help you take the first step toward defining your values and morals. I have included an abbreviated version of the exercise below.

The Four Corners Exercise

The four corners represent various degrees of unethical behavior from not a problem to seriously wrong.

1) Not a problem (Integrity remains intact.)	**3) Kind of wrong** (Moderate compromise of integrity.)
2) Everybody does it (Minor compromise of integrity.)	**4) Seriously wrong** (Critical compromise of integrity.)

Consider the following ethical dilemmas. Indicate your response to each by writing the question letter in one of four corners above. Do not read the evaluation of any item until you have provided a response for all items.

A. You accept a job offer, signing the contract on Monday to start in two weeks. The following week, you receive an offer from another company where you had interviewed at nearly the same time. They offer you a higher salary and more responsibility. You take the new job and rescind your previous acceptance just two days prior to your start date.

B. You are riding the train to work, as you do most workdays. The conductor comes by but does not take your ticket. You take advantage of the free ride and use the same ticket the following day.

C. You are paying for your groceries at the supermarket when you notice that the cashier has given you $20 too much in change. Rather than handing it back, you pocket the extra bill.

D. You are working for a high-tech company. One day, your boss asks you to call a competitor to get information about a new product in development there. He tells you not to mention that you are working for this company, but rather to say that you are a student in an MBA program gathering data for a report. You decide to do as your boss says.

Now that you have marked your initial response to each dilemma consider how these added details might affect your answers. Based on this new information, would you move your answer to a different corner?

A. You made a commitment to the initial job, but you vastly prefer to work at the new job. The company and the position are more in line with your interests. On the other hand, a dear friend helped you get the interview at the company whose offer you already had accepted. Not only would you hurt her feelings if you reneged on your acceptance, but also your actions might cause her boss to lose faith in her.

B. The train you ride to work every day is part of a giant corporation with annual earnings in the millions. Many times
when you paid the full fare, the train was late and you suffered the consequences at work. You wonder that maybe
the company owes you a free ride at this point.

C. The cashier is a single mom of 35, struggling to make ends
meet. She will have to pay for her mistake (handing you
the extra $20 bill) out of her own pocket. As a result, she
will have to cut certain important expenses this month.

D. You are completing a three-month internship with the
high-tech company. If you don't lie to the competitor about
your identity, as your boss asked, you will not receive an
offer for full-time employment when the internship ends.

As you evaluate your responses, consider the following
questions:

1. Did you change a response due to the specific nature of
the added details—for example, because the cashier now
seems needier, while the train company is more deserving
of being ripped off? In other words, did the "humanity" of
the situation influence your response?

2. What if everyone in the situations described above acted
as you had in these fictional scenarios? For example, what
if people were constantly making calls to competitors posing as researchers to gain access to confidential information? Would your decision change if you knew that your
act would set a precedent that many other people would
follow?

3. Would your decision change if you had to tell your mother,
your best friend, and your colleagues what you had done?

4. Would your decision change if you knew you would have
to answer to the person who suffered as a result?

Note that the point of Four Corners is not to establish right versus wrong answers, but rather for you to deepen your understanding of your own thought processes and judge whether you are being fair and consistent. Engaging in the Four Corners exercise helps to identify what your Platinum Standard is and tests your commitment to it.

For instance, one of my students changed his mind about re-using his train ticket after a class discussion. At first he stood in the "Everybody does it" corner. But after talking about the integrity of that choice, he changed his mind to "Seriously wrong." The discussion helped him realize that re-using his ticket was the equivalent of stealing. Even if the train company were large and not heavily impacted by one person stealing one ticket, that would not make the behavior acceptable. When acting with integrity, you must ask yourself the following questions:

1. Would I want this done to me? The likely answer is no.
2. What if everyone did what I did? The whole system would break down.

After class, the student said, "I learned that if I used the same ticket the next day, I would be creating a troubling precedent that threatened the essence of the ethics of all my actions."

In the case of taking the extra change, an executive in one of my corporate trainings who initially said, "It's not a problem," changed his mind to "It's seriously wrong" when he learned that the cashier was a single mother. After a discussion of the exercise, however, he realized that he was not acting consistently. Altering his behavior due to the cashier's personal circumstances was equivalent to giving one employee a bigger bonus simply because he connected with that person better than the others under his supervision. The essence of integrity is treating all people according to the same standards that you have set for yourself.

The executive said, "This exercise taught me that when you act consistently, people will consistently trust you."

In summary, Me Power involves getting in touch with our inner divinity placed in all of us by God. It includes evaluating our Spiritual Fitness as outlined in Chapter 1, straightening out crooked thinking as discussed in Chapter 2, and understanding our integrity standards (our Platinum Standard) in this chapter. This prepares us to bring forth our best self—Me Power—as we deal and interact with others—We Power.

We Power

We Power recognizes that we live interdependent lives. As Christians, we are the Body of Christ with Jesus as the Head of the Church. Unlike Me Power, which is internal, We Power is an outward power. The focus shifts from individual to community.

We Power is a multiplier. It is greater than the sum of all Me Powers. It requires that we give, receive, and collaborate to fully achieve our incredible human potential and, with God's assistance, build His kingdom on earth.

In this Part, you discover practical ways to increase We Power in your life, including

- Establishing and maintaining a peaceful coexistence
- Living in service to others
- Building more personal and more meaningful relationships

CHAPTER 4

Peaceful Coexistence

Me Power involves getting in touch with our inner divinity. This prepares us to bring forth our best selves
as we deal and interact with others to fully realize
our We Power.

We Power recognizes that we live interdependent lives. As
our Christian faith tells us, we are all connected as one part of
one unified body—the Body of Christ.

We Power is an outward power. It is about giving to and receiving from others and requires that we not only tolerate but
actually love one another.

Jesus instructed us to, "Love your neighbor as yourself." It's
relatively easy to love our family and friends, but we're asked to
do more. The give and take of "We" involves the world at large.
Consider the following statement by Pope Francis during a recent TED Talk:

> Each and everyone's existence is deeply tied to
> that of others; life is not time merely passing by,
> life is about interactions.
>
> We all need each other; none of us is an island,
> an autonomous and independent "I," separated
> from the other, and we can only build the future
> by standing together, including everyone. We
> don't think about it often, but everything is con-

nected, and we need to restore our connections
to a healthy state. Even the harsh judgment I hold
in my heart against my brother or sister, the open
wound that was never cured, the offense that was
never forgiven, the rancor that is only going to
hurt me—are all instances of a fight that I carry
within me, a flare deep in my heart that needs to
be extinguished before it goes up in flames, leaving only ashes behind.

Many of us, nowadays, seem to believe that a
happy future is something impossible to achieve.
While such concerns must be taken very seriously, they are not invincible. They can be overcome when we don't lock our door to the outside
world. Happiness can only be discovered as a gift
of harmony between the whole and each single
component.

When Jesus was asked what the greatest commandment was,
He replied, "Love the Lord your God with all your heart and with
all your soul and with all your mind. This is the first and greatest
commandment. And the second is like it: Love your neighbor as
yourself. All the Law and the Prophets hang on these two commandments" (Matthew 22:37–40 NIV).

Loving our family and friends is relatively easy, but we're
asked to do more. As you're aware, Jesus was not talking only
about the residents in our neighborhoods or even those in our
extended networks. He was speaking universally—in a sense, everyone on the planet is our neighbor.

Barriers to Loving Our Neighbors

Loving our neighbors is often difficult due to several barriers that stand in our way—self-preservation, suspicion, selfishness, tribalism, ignorance, and so on. These factors often give rise to biases (conscious and subconscious), stereotypes, and prejudice. Add fear to the mix, and we have the foundation for distrust and hatred. We fear what we don't understand and cling to the familiar. In the words of Rabbi Lord Jonathan Sacks:

> We're surrounded almost entirely by people like us whose views, whose opinions, whose prejudices, even, are just like ours. And Cass Sunstein of Harvard has shown that if we surround ourselves with people with the same views as us, we get more extreme. I think we need to renew those face-to-face encounters with the people not like us. I think we need to do that in order to realize that we can disagree strongly and yet still stay friends.
>
> It's in those face-to-face encounters that we discover that the people not like us are just people, like us. And actually, every time we hold out the hand of friendship to somebody not like us, whose class or creed or color are different from ours, we heal one of the fractures of our wounded world.

I know the dangers of provincialism first hand. I grew up in a bubble. I was raised in Weston, Connecticut, which is about an hour away from New York City. The population at the time was about 10,000. Out of the 100 or so kids in my grade, there were only two non-white classmates—a "Mexican" and an "Indian" (we didn't use culturally sensitive language back then). Although

I don't recall either of them being teased or bullied, neither of them really assimilated, and they more or less kept to themselves. All I remember is that they were different from anyone I had ever seen. They dressed, spoke, and looked different.

About a year later, a family moved into town from China. In this case, "Tami" was an outgoing kid eager to make friends. I enjoyed getting to know him and learning about Chinese culture. However, when he invited me to his birthday party, I was a little nervous at first. I wondered what kind of games we'd play and whether there would be a birthday cake (there was). His parents and siblings were very friendly, and everyone had a great time. Even though this was my first experience with a Chinese family, I recall thinking, "Hmm, they're not so different than the rest of us." In fact, I thought it was kind of cool having a friend from the other side of the world.

My world expanded even further when our class took a trip to the Bronx Zoo. It was 1969. When our bus pulled into the parking lot, I noticed dozens of other buses from inner city schools. As the kids exited the buses, I was astonished by what I saw—hundreds of "colored" kids (back then the term "colored" was in common use by both black and white people). Today, of course, we use either "black" or "African-American."

As a side note, a few years ago I was doing consulting work for the Chief Diversity Officer of a global advertising firm, who was black. Not wanting to offend her, and in the spirit of opening discussion, I told her I was somewhat confused about the difference between "black" and "African-American." I wasn't sure which term I should use and under what circumstances. She appreciated the query and explained that the term "African-American" is used for those who are first generation Africans living now in America. She further explained that "black" is used for those who are second generation and beyond U.S. citizens.

Seeing large groups of kids who looked so different than my friends in the Weston bubble was fascinating. I was too young to understand the state of race relations and the Civil Rights Movement going on at the time. Thankfully, I was raised in an environment where we were taught to treat all people with respect. Therefore, I did not harbor any prejudice or have any preconceived notions regarding race.

Gradually, my world opened up. It busted wide open when I decided to backpack for three weeks across Europe. Until that point, I had never been out of the country. I had experienced differences in cultures but only within the U.S. My journey took me through about 12 countries. Along the way, I met dozens of young people from all over the world.

I stayed in youth hostels and B&Bs (this was decades before Airbnb). Travel was mostly via Eurorail (known today as Eurail). As a result, I had the opportunity to really get to know my fellow travelers, especially on long train rides and hanging out in the hostels. It was amazing how well we got along with each other in spite of our language differences. Regardless of nationality, I believe we connected so well because we were sharing a common experience. We were strangers in a strange, or different, land.

Challenge: Open yourself up to a new or different point of view. Seek out those with a worldview that differs from yours and engage them in dialogue. Hold judgment and don't be too quick to offer a rebuttal. Find areas of agreement and common ground.

Challenge: Open yourself up to a new or different point of view. Seek out those with a worldview that differs from yours and engage them in dialogue.

Hold judgment and don't be too quick to offer a rebuttal. Find areas of agreement and common ground.

Peaceful coexistence becomes a reality when we realize that we all share a common bond. As Christians, that common bond is God the Father, and we are his children. Yes, that means we're brothers and sisters. And just as it is with our siblings in our own families, we at times don't get along. We argue, fight, and sometimes become estranged for long periods of time. This is all part of our common humanity. But Jesus admonishes us not only to love our neighbor but to love our enemies as well. For me, this is the most difficult aspect of Christianity.

Peaceful coexistence does not mean that we have to like one another or agree in order to avoid conflict. In today's polarized society it seems that people can't express disagreement or opposing views in a civil, respectful manner. Most often, debate and disagreement quickly devolve into both a verbal and (sometimes) physical brawl. Again, we must look to Jesus as our role model. He was attacked verbally and physically by people who vehemently disagreed with teachings considered radical and even heretical. But through it all, he kept his cool. That doesn't mean that he remained silent or avoided contentious issues, far from it. He always responded, but he did so firmly, directly, and rationally.

For example, here's how Jesus handled a question designed to trap him and invoke the wrath of the Roman government:

> Then the Pharisees went out and laid plans to trap him in his words. They sent their disciples to him along with the Herodians. "Teacher," they said, "we know that you are a man of integrity and that you teach the way of God in accordance with the truth. You aren't swayed by others, because you pay no attention to who they are. Tell us then,

what is your opinion? Is it right to pay the imperial tax to Caesar or not?"

But Jesus, knowing their evil intent, said, "You
hypocrites, why are you trying to trap me? Show
me the coin used for paying the tax." They brought
him a denarius, and he asked them, "Whose image is this? And whose inscription?"

"Caesar's," they replied.

Then he said to them, "So give back to Caesar
what is Caesar's, and to God what is God's." When
they heard this, they were amazed. So they left
him and went away (Matthew 22:15-22 NIV).

First of all, Jesus was on to their shenanigans. This was a hot
button issue with the Jews. The imperial tax was levied on subjects (including the Jews) but not Roman citizens. If Jesus says
"yes," it is right to pay the imperial tax, He could anger the Jewish
people who would likely perceive the answer to be in support
of the Roman oppression. If He says "no," the Pharisees can ac-
cuse Jesus of being a revolutionary against Rome. So, Jesus calls
them out on their deception and shuts down the controversy,
thus avoiding retribution by the Romans and honoring God—all
in one profound sentence!

The main point here is that peaceful coexistence does not
mean that we remain silent in the midst of evil or injustice.
Voicing an opinion or even passionately disagreeing with an opposing viewpoint is not only acceptable but also obligatory in
certain situations. However, we must always comport ourselves
in a dignified and respectful manner no matter how much we
may disagree. The key is how we go about it.

Tips for Respectful Disagreement
• Allow the other person to speak first.
• Do not interrupt.
• Do not attack.
• Seek to truly understand.
• Clarify your interpretation.
• Express your point of view.
• Be measured in your tone.
• Avoid using personal insults.
• Seek common ground when possible.
• Agree to disagree if necessary.

"Supreme" Coexistence

Given today's intense political and social environment, we can learn how to handle disagreements by examining how two Supreme Court justices managed to peacefully coexist. Ruth Bader Ginsburg and the late Antonin Scalia couldn't have been further apart ideologically, yet they shared a strong friendship going as far back as the 1980s. They bonded over a mutual love for opera, good food, and travel and refused to let their professional disagreements undermine their personal friendship. The following is an excerpt from a 2016 story appearing in The Washington Post:

> "If you can't disagree ardently with your colleagues about some issues of law and yet personally still be friends, get another job, for Pete's sake," is how Scalia once described their lifetime appointments. "As annoyed as you might be about his zinging dissent, he's so utterly charming, so amusing, so sometimes outrageous, you can't help

but say, 'I'm glad that he's my friend or he's my colleague,' " Ginsburg said. Sometimes, she said, she had to pinch herself to not laugh in the court-room when Scalia said something audacious.

I admire the fact that despite their ideological differences and heated debates, the justices had mutual respect for one another and a genuine friendship borne out of love. We can learn a great deal from their example.

Treat Others as You'd Like to Be Treated

Yes, Jesus admonished us to love our neighbor, and we all know the Golden Rule: Treat others as you'd like to be treated. This is well-illustrated in the story of the Good Samaritan who stumbles across a man on the side of the road, badly beaten and bruised. Others traveling the same road before him walked right by with complete indifference to the suffering of a fellow human being. But the Good Samaritan showed great compassion (which comes from loving big), bringing the injured man to a nearby inn to treat his wounds and provide a safe and comfortable place to convalesce. He covers all expenses and promises the innkeeper that he will pay any additional costs associated with the victim's recovery.

Here's the kicker: the stranger was a Jew. At that time, Samaritans hated the Jews and vice versa. Yet, the Good Samaritan saw only a fellow human being in need. He didn't care whether the stranger was rich or poor. He didn't inquire about political beliefs or views on current events. He simply took care of his neighbor and treated him with respect and compassion.

I'm sure you are familiar with Mother Teresa of Calcutta, who passed away in 1997. She started an order called the Missionaries of Charity, which is a Roman Catholic religious congregation. As a Catholic nun serving in Calcutta, India, her mission was simple:

to serve the poorest of the poor, which included enabling those near death to die with dignity.

In 1952, Teresa opened her first hospice. She and the nuns of her order would literally lift the dying out of the gutter and bring them back to the home. While there, they received medical attention and the opportunity to die with dignity in accordance with their faith: Muslims were read the Quran, Hindus received water from the Ganges, and Catholics received the Sacrament known as the Anointing of the Sick. The Missionaries of Charity had been practicing the Platinum Rule (treat others as they would like to be treated) long before the Platinum Rule was published. "A beautiful death," Teresa said, "is for people who lived like animals to die like angels—loved and wanted."

As a Catholic, I am well aware that Mother Teresa was a controversial figure. She was a standard bearer of Catholic doctrine, which didn't sit well with many people. Though she held fast to her views, she kept to her mission, which was equal opportunity. She never judged—race, religion, political affiliation, lifestyle— none of that mattered. She saw every individual as a child of God. This is tolerance in the truest sense of the word. Unfortunately, all too often, people confuse tolerance with accepting or condoning certain behaviors, even sinful behavior. However, we must be careful to distinguish between tolerance and allowance.

Who Will Throw the First Stone?

The story of Jesus and the adulterous woman serves as an excellent example of how we can be tolerant of people without accepting or condoning their behavior:

> Jesus returned to the Mount of Olives, but early the next morning he was back again at the Temple. A crowd soon gathered, and he sat down and taught them. As he was speaking, the teachers of

religious law and the Pharisees brought a woman who had been caught in the act of adultery. They put her in front of the crowd.

"Teacher," they said to Jesus, "this woman was caught in the act of adultery. The Law of Moses says to stone her. What do you say?" They were trying to trap him into saying something they could use against him, but Jesus stooped down and wrote in the dust with his finger.

They kept demanding an answer, so he stood up again and said, "All right, but let the one who has never sinned throw the first stone!" Then he stooped down again and wrote in the dust.

When the accusers heard this, they slipped away one by one, beginning with the oldest, until only Jesus was left in the middle of the crowd with the woman. Then Jesus stood up again and said to the woman, "Where are your accusers? Didn't even one of them condemn you?" "No, Lord," she said. And Jesus said, "Neither do I. Go and sin no more" (John 8:1-11 NLT).

A couple of important points here: First, Jesus in essence is saying, "Before you punish someone else for committing a sinful act, be sure your own hands are clean." Too often we see people condemning others when their own behavior is far worse. Second, and this is an important point, Jesus was in no way saying that adultery was not a sin. Remember, His last words to her were, "Go and sin no more."

The lesson for us Christians is that we should not be too quick to judge or condemn. Peaceful coexistence is threatened when we condemn or marginalize people for behavior we deem sinful. If we were to spend more time examining our own shortcomings, we would have less time and be less inclined to point out the faults of others. At the same time, we need to recognize that sin is real and is harmful—some more so than others. We need to love one another while we reject sinful behavior: "Hate the sin but love the sinner." For example, I think abortion is wrong, a violation of the sixth commandment, Thou shall not kill. In my view, the taking of an innocent life is a grave sin. At the same time, I know that some people do not consider an embryo or a fetus a living being or they think that a women's right to choose overrides the baby's right to live. I know that for many women, the decision to abort is heart-wrenching.

Many who go through with it are tormented by their decision and later come to regret the choice they made. Some cannot forgive themselves.

Here's my point: I recognize abortion as a grave sin, and I'm not afraid to speak out on the subject in a civil manner. At the same time, I'm in no position to judge or condemn a person—that's God's business. I don't believe in publicly shaming people who support abortion. I don't believe in blowing up abortion clinics. Violence only begets more violence. When two sides of an opposing viewpoint or ideology resort to violence, the driver is hate. That's in direct violation of Jesus' admonition to love our neighbor (as well as our enemies!). Therein lies the key to peaceful coexistence.

CHAPTER 5

Serving Others

Faith requires that we go out into the world to share our gifts with others—also known as "faith in action." As Jesus said, "Let your light so shine before men, that they may see your good works and glorify your Father which is in heaven" (Matthew 5:16 KJV). When thinking about serving others, I've found it useful to use an analogy we are all familiar with.

The Customer Concept

Jesus admonishes us to love our neighbor. For illustrative purposes, let's think of our neighbor as a *customer*. I realize that the term "customer" sounds cold and impersonal when referring to people with whom we have relationships outside of the workplace, but it provides a powerful mental model. Think for a moment about how you treat your customers in business:

- They're your top priority—they're the reason you exist.
- You are sensitive to their needs, problems, and concerns.
- You consistently deliver high-quality goods and services to please them.
- You have a vested interest in their success.
- You address problems quickly.
- You know that if you don't deliver quality you risk losing them to the competition.

- You're always looking for creative, new ways of "wowing" your customers—it's a never-ending process.

The word "customer" has become part of our everyday vernacular in business. Customer-focused companies put people before profits because they know that if they take care of the customer, higher revenues, market share, and profits will follow.

Adopting the customer mindset outside of the workplace serves as a conscious reminder that we should always be thinking of our customers. Understanding the origin of the word "customer" helps to reinforce this point. Here's a story as told by a professor friend:

> I was driving along with the quandary of a course idea for my next management course. Public radio was on in the background, and there was a radio play on the air. It took place in Early American times, here in New England. I listened more intently as a young gentleman rode to a nearby village to go to a bootmaker. He needed to replace a pair of riding boots made in his own town that had never fit well and wore out too soon. There was a brief interchange with the bootmaker who was as skillful with his questions as he might be with his needle. This craftsman was acting as though he needed to know a great deal from the potential customer. This was not a "give me a size ten" shoe store. These would be custom-made. The cobbler gleaned information on the nature of his horses, how he intended to ride, what his preferences were for the color of his clothing—information elicited with friendly, yet purposeful dialogue. I could hear the cobbler's genuine interest

in the actor's portrayal. It was as if he were eager
to make boots for this man and his descendants!

The gentleman must have heard it too, for he
said, "Bootmaker, you have shown me what
your unfortunate competitor in my village
could not. Therefore, I plight thee my custom."
Here he was giving the cobbler his trust and
permission to labor over a pair of boots with
exacting knowledge of their "fitness for use."
That cobbler/actor solved *my* problem in that
same instant. I made a point of the next course to
be to learn how to earn, give, and use "custom" as
the true stuff of organizational success.

Look at the word "customer." You'll see that it contains another word inside of it: "custom." The word "customer" literally
means the "giver of custom"—a promise of regular patronage to
a particular shop, restaurant, or other business. Custom was offered as an honor and a bond of trust, and it could be taken away
at any time as an act of rejection. If this transaction were put into
words, it could be expressed like this: "Promise quality and I will
give you my 'custom' from which your product and service can
be fashioned." Ponder the magnitude of the act of giving and uti-
lizing of custom. Does it not represent the most elemental force
of business? To give one's custom is to form a bond of business.
To take it away is to remove business—for one customer or many.

In the MBA class I teach at Fordham University, I drive home
this point by asking my students to take out a blank sheet of paper and sign their name to it. Then, using the language from the
bootmaker story, I ask them to swap it with another student's as
they say, "I plight thee my custom." I instruct them to examine
their partner's signature. Then I tell them, "Our signatures are

unique and personal—something most of us take great pride in. Handwriting analysts claim that it reveals something about our personalities, or who we are. In a sense, our signature is 'custom fit'."

After that, I instruct them to crumble up their partner's signed paper and toss it back to them. I ask them to open up their "custom" and describe how they feel. Their responses are often filled with anger, resentment, rejection, and disappointment:

"I feel violated."

"It was disrespectful."

"I'm hurt."

"I expected better treatment."

I conclude the exercise by saying, "This is exactly what happens when we don't deliver on our commitment to quality with our customers."

This is what I want you to think about as you reflect on the word "customer" for use beyond the workplace. I use the word "customer" to describe meaningful relationships. Imagine what life would be like if you treated the people you encounter in life as you treat your customers in business. It is a powerful reminder that the people you come into contact with on a regular basis, whether at home, work, school, on the streets, or any other place, are human beings with special needs and wants. Keep in mind that if you don't take care of your customer's needs and wants, they'll take their "business" elsewhere. The cost of losing customers is high. It can be tallied in how it manifests itself— broken relationships, estrangement, separation, divorce, and so on. Cultivating and nourishing your customer relationships is a big step towards "loving your neighbor."

Who Are Our Customers?

As businesses have discovered, identifying one's customers can be quite complicated. One of my most interesting and challenging consulting assignments involved a well-known fast food chain headquartered in the Northeast. I was asked to facilitate a process improvement project in one of their outlets. During a meeting with management and key staff, I asked the question, "Who are your customers?"

An arm quickly shot up from a cashier who said, "Our customers are the people who come into the store to purchase our product."

Then one of the bakers chimed in and said, "The purchaser is not *my* customer. My customer is the person who prepares the sandwich."

Then the person in charge of catering said, "My customer is the individual representing corporations who phones in large catering orders."

At this point, they were beginning to understand that their customers were actually like a cast of characters playing various roles, each representing a unique set of needs and demands to be met. Upon closer investigation, the group found that their customers could be broken down into different "classes" based on their level of importance and complexity of needs. For instance, the catering customer was considered to be more valuable than the individual walk-in customer. Within the catering class of customer were subclasses that could also be ranked in order of importance. Suppose the VP of Sales was hosting a lunch meeting for her sales reps. Chances are she would not personally place the order. Instead, she might delegate the task to her administrative assistant. The receptionist would receive the delivery, the reps would eat the food, and the VP of Sales would pay for it. Suddenly, the customer list grows from one to four, each of which has a different set of needs. To ensure quality, the caterer must understand the distinct needs of each class and subclass of customers.

Identify Your Customers

We, too, have many customers in our personal lives—some obvious, others not so obvious. Take a moment now to brainstorm a list of *your* customers. Think about the roles you play in life, as well as the activities you're involved in, and list all the people you come in contact with on a regular basis. List everybody you can think of—don't leave anybody out—and be creative. Your list might include:

God, self, spouse, children, significant other, parents, friends, acquaintances, relatives, roommate(s), boss, coworkers, employees, landlord, fellow citizens, commuters, public service officials, teachers, and so on.

Compare your list to the people on your Christmas card list—have you forgotten anybody?

Classify and Rank Your Customers

After listing your customers, rank them by class. Admittedly, ranking customers, especially those in our personal lives, may seem cold and calculating. Jesus did say, "As I have loved you, so you must love one another" (John 13:34 BSB). Yet, none of us has infinite time and energy to serve the needs of others, and not all customers require the same level of care and feeding. Given our limited human resources, we need to prioritize and allocate. We can't be all things to all people.

Think about how much time and energy you invest in managing your different customer relationships. You may find that you are spending an inordinate amount of time with a particular customer at the expense of another with greater needs. Or, you may discover that you are "spinning your wheels"—investing resources without achieving the desired level of customer satisfaction. Your assessment of what a certain customer really needs may be mistaken.

Managing customers and meeting their needs can become quite unwieldy without the proper assessments and organization.

I've found that as I grow older, my list of customers has grown, and their needs have become more complex. Every now and then, I must assess my growing customer base, reclassify my customers, and prioritize around their changing needs.

You can rank your customers, using a variety of methods. Some people use precious metals as their categories: Platinum, Gold, Silver, and Bronze. Others use A, B, C, and D. I recommend four broad categories—God and Self, Vital Few, Important Several, and Useful Many—but I encourage you to be creative. Use whatever strikes your fancy, and have some fun with it. What's important is that your system is meaningful to you.

One word of caution: I don't recommend sharing your classification system with your customers. You want to avoid hurting someone's feelings who hasn't made your "A" list.

God and Self

The first and highest priority class of customers has two members—God and self. God is first because Jesus tells us so: "Love the Lord your God with all your heart and with all your soul and with all your mind. This is the first and greatest commandment" (Matthew 22:37–38 NIV). The reason God is our top priority customer is that God made us, and "with God, all things are possible" (Matthew 19:26). As explained in Part 1 of this book, our relationship with God is essential for optimizing our Me Power.

Second only to God is self, which might surprise you. The logic is similar to that employed by flight attendants when reminding passengers, "In the event of a loss of cabin pressure, oxygen masks will automatically drop down from the compartment above your head. Pull the mask down toward your face and place the mask over your mouth and nose. For those traveling with children, please be sure to secure your mask first, then your child's." We can't take care of our customers unless we first take good care of ourselves. Do you take better care of your customers than of yourself? Caring for yourself is not a selfish act—it is an implementation of Me Power that enables you to actively pursue We Power.

Recall that Jesus often went off by himself to a solitary place to pray. He recognized the need to be alone with His Father for spiritual replenishment and refreshment in preparation for His demanding work of serving others. He knew He needed Me Power to engage with and begin to build a community of followers to help build the Kingdom of God on earth. In essence, Jesus was serving his two highest priority customers first—God, the Father, and Himself.

Vital Few

The vital few are those with whom you have the closest relationship. You interact with them on a frequent, if not daily, basis. They are your top priority. These are the people indirectly responsible for your happiness, well-being, and fulfillment in life. They are the people you depend on regularly when you need a shoulder to cry on, someone to share your joy with, or someone to turn to when you need advice on an important matter. You drop everything when they need you.

I think of a business executive friend of mine who traveled extensively for his job. One day while on business in California, he called his teenage daughter to "check in." When asked, "How's everything?" she could barely respond; something had upset her to the point of tears. Sensing that this was more than just the usual "day-in-the-life of a teenager" dilemma, he immediately dropped everything and got on the next plane east to be with her.

Sometimes the vital few customers are the ones we take most for granted. I'm sure you've heard of the old Mills Brothers' song "You Always Hurt the One You Love." We usually hurt those close to us when we take them for granted and stop treating them as our most valued customers—when we ignore their needs. Yet, these are the very people who should be our top priority, second only to God. Even Jesus had a clear understanding of His "vital few," which I believe first and foremost was God the Father followed by his 12 disciples.

Important Several
The important several are the people in your life with whom you have occasional, but ongoing, contact—whether through work, school, or outside activities (clubs, sports, groups, organizations, etc.) The relationship is casual but important enough to monitor its quality.

Useful Many
The useful many are the people in our lives with whom we have random or sporadic contact. They may include people you know on a first-name basis: your postal carrier, babysitter, waiter, hair stylist, gas station attendant, bank teller, and so on. Also among the useful many are the nameless, sometimes faceless, people we meet briefly or never at all. They represent the world at large—humanity.

The Law of Supply and Demand
Years ago, the customer ranking system became an invaluable tool to my wife, Catherine, and me when we were compiling our list of wedding attendees. We brainstormed a long list of possible guests—including family members, old high school friends, college buddies, distant relatives, colleagues, coworkers, and so on. Being from a large Italian-Catholic family didn't help. Since we were paying for the reception ourselves, we had to pare the list down considerably. We sorted the list into the three categories and made our final picks. This was very difficult for us because we wanted everybody on our long list to attend. We also knew that the people dropped from the list might never want to associate with us again. As it turned out, it was a useful exercise—we were able to winnow the list to fit our budget. It also reminded us how quickly our customer list had grown. Unlike in business,

most of our customers in life stay with us, demanding different levels of attention. I believe it's perfectly appropriate, if not critical, to occasionally review our list of customers and pare back where necessary. Managing our lives is a lot like running a business. It comes down to economics—the allocation of limited resources. We have a fixed amount of resources in terms of time, money, energy, attention, and so on, but the demands placed on us by our customers are not fixed.

When organizations bring on more customers, they make additional investments in infrastructure to ensure they can meet the associated demands.

We have no such luxury in our personal lives. We can, of course, make better use of our resources by becoming more efficient, and we can leverage our relationships to make better use of shared resources, but we ultimately encounter certain limitations. Therefore, it becomes incumbent upon us to actively manage the influx of new customers and the demands of existing customers, lest we become stretched too thin. When we are stretched too thin, we wind up providing only mediocre levels of "customer service" and no one is happy. By reassessing our relationships on a regular basis, we ensure that everyone on our list, including ourselves, receives the appropriate level of customer service.

Quantity vs. Quality

Some people have many friends and acquaintances. A few I know have a thousand or more friends on Facebook (quantity), but, for the most part, the relationships are shallow and superficial (poor quality). We are social animals and want to interact with, and be liked by, others. It's a very reasonable and important need, as long as we don't get too carried away. Managing more than a handful of important relationships, though, is difficult. Any manager in business knows that she can effectively manage only a limited number of direct reports—approximately seven to ten. Any more than that and she is less effective.

If you're actively serving more than a dozen customers regularly, consider reducing the number, or at least creating some distance between you and them. Of course, you must be compassionate and diplomatic when whittling down your list, but for your sake and the sake of your most valued customers, you need to budget yourself. Quality relationships demand substantial investment. You may have people on your list who sap you of your energy and spirit. We all have certain customers who intrude regularly on our lives and who may be pursuing only their own self-interests. Parting ways may be best for you and them; you may have unwittingly formed a codependency that's unhealthy for you and your customer. Reducing your list will free up resources, enabling you to increase both the quantity and quality of time with your vital few customers.

Expanding Your Resources

Although each of us is limited in respect to the number of customers we serve and the level of service we provide, we can expand our resources to a certain degree. Once again, we turn to Jesus as an example. Everywhere Jesus traveled, He was followed by large crowds looking for miracles and healing. This led to His authorizing the disciples to join him in the work that needed to be done. Instead of trying to fly solo, as many of us attempt to do, Jesus carefully trained his disciples and entrusted them with some of the work. In so doing, Jesus provided a prime example of how to multiply Me Power through the use of We Power.

As you become more customer-centric in your life, look for ways to conserve and expand your resources. Here are a few ideas to spark your own creativity:

- Delegate like Jesus did. Hire an assistant or take on an intern. An assistant is anyone who does work that you would normally do yourself, such as organizing your office, cleaning your house, or mowing the lawn.

- Empower your customers. Many of your "needy" customers are likely to benefit from becoming more self-sufficient. Good parents, for example, teach their children how to perform tasks instead of doing everything for them.
- Learn and develop more efficient methods for conducting your daily activities. This may include learning new technologies or investing in machines that automate or simplify certain tasks.
- Make conscious decisions about where to invest your time and energy. Non-productive activities, such as watching TV, are okay in small doses, but those activities can easily consume our waking hours if we're not careful.

Understanding Customer Needs

We keep our vitally important customers by being responsive, if not proactive, in meeting and exceeding their needs. After you've identified and prioritized your customers, the real work begins—discovering their needs and finding ways to consistently deliver on them. How do we discover customer needs? One obvious way is to ask them, but that is not always the best method. Many customers don't know what they want or cannot articulate their needs.

The following sections present three methods that can be used in conjunction with one another to identify a customer's needs: Pulse Check Survey, Interview, and Observation.

Pulse Check Survey

Losing touch with people we are close to is far too easy; we get busy and preoccupied with other tasks or interests, or we simply get distracted. Modern life is full of distractions.

We assume that as long as our important customers seem satisfied, everything must be fine, but that's a risky assumption when your goal is customer retention and satisfaction. Dissatisfied customers often leave with little or no warning. Repeated irritations, neglect, slights, and errant words, build up and fester over time. The pulse check survey can provide early warning of potential problems, enabling you to prevent customer dissatisfaction pro- actively. It can also provide valuable information on how to delight your customer.

First, identify which customer you want to survey. This is an important first step because you want to customize the survey to fit the customer and the situation. Then design a survey than can be easily followed and administered. The following is an example of a survey I use with my university students at the end of each semester. My preference is to use a numeric scale (1–5) to get a better handle on the intensity of their position. I think it's important to ascertain their overall sentiment (see the first question below) as well as their views on specific aspects of the class. Notice also that I allow room on the survey for students to add specific qualitative comments.

Survey Form

Please indicate how strongly you agree with each of the following statements on a scale from 1 to 5:

1	2	3	4	5
Not at all		Somewhat		Very much

	1	2	3	4	5
The class met my expectations.					
The essays were helpful.					
The team meetings were helpful.					
The class discussions were helpful.					

The lectures were helpful.					
The handouts were helpful.					
I will apply what I've learned.					

Which concepts did you like most?

Which concepts did you like the least?

What changes (if any) would you make to the course?

Would you recommend this course to a friend? (Please check one.): Yes ____ No ____

Additional Comments:

This format can be modified for use with *any* customer or customers: spouse, children, boss, peers, friends, family, etc. Frame your questions around specific interest areas. Be clear about what kind of information you're looking for.

For instance, if you're trying to be a better spouse, you might develop questions specific to issues or concerns relating to how you manage finances, handle disagreements, raise the children, spend your free time, etc.

The Survey as an Initiation Device

The survey serves as a tool to initiate communication between you and your customer. The biggest cause of separation and divorce is lack of communication. People either don't have the time or don't know how or what to communicate. A user-friendly survey triggers communication in a fun and playful way. Think about it. We all love to be asked our opinion—we especially love giving our opinion.

Don't forget that the "customer" concept is a useful metaphor. Don't approach the survey or the discussion around it as a cold, impersonal business transaction. Your questions should be warm, personal, and deeply sincere. Your most valuable customers will appreciate your desire to improve the quality of the relationship. I suggest giving your customer time to complete the survey, without you present. Give them time to reflect on your questions and provide thoughtful responses. If you are surveying many people, I suggest using email if possible or a free online survey tool, such as SurveyMonkey. After you've reviewed the response(s), decide what you want to do next. More than likely, you'll want details not necessarily provided in the survey response. If that's the case, *schedule* a face-to-face meeting or interview to probe deeper and seek clarity.

Interview
Whether preceded by a survey or not, an interview is a great way to facilitate dialogue between you and your customer. Just as with creating a survey, you'll want to be well prepared for your interview.

Compose the questions you want to ask and arrange them in the desired sequence. Send the questions to your customer, in advance. At this point, you may be thinking, "This guy is nuts. I'm not going to interview my husband, wife, child, boss, or friend. These are human beings, not business associates!" I agree that it sounds a little crazy, but it actually makes a lot of sense. The interview serves as a facilitation mechanism—a formal, unbiased approach to guide the dialogue between you and your customer.

Think about the last time you tried to have a constructive, meaningful discussion with someone important in your life. How did it go? We usually avoid touchy or sensitive topics, or we lose our focus and start rambling without any sense of purpose or direction. Many times, unguided discussions spin out of control and descend into finger-pointing or shouting matches. Interviews guided with well thought-out questions depersonalize the dialogue, thus leading to constructive outcomes. The interview method is especially important in that it puts communication on the *agenda*. If it's not scheduled, it probably won't happen. What is the quality of your communication as you're running out the door for work or at the end of a long, hectic day? Introducing structure and formality into the communication process on occasion is a good thing.

Observation

Sometimes we learn most about our customers by studying their behavior and habits. Customers don't always know what they need or express their needs in ways that are vague or confusing.

One of my clients, a personal computer (PC) manufacturer, regularly invites prospective customers (end users) to actually try out new product concepts or existing products slated for improvement. End users are ushered into a large room filled with PCs and asked to try them out. Researchers and product developers observe user behavior from behind a one-way glass, taking copious notes. They're primarily interested in seeing how the product is actually used (unintended use) compared to its design (intended use). This process gives them valuable input into the product design process.

The frisbee was thought of years ago by a clever employee of the Frisbee Pie Co., located at the time in Bridgeport, Connecticut. He observed that each day during lunch break, his co-workers would toss empty pie tins to pass the time. The pie tins back then were very durable (not like the flimsy aluminum ones that accompany today's frozen pies and pie crusts) and were capable of flying long distances. An entire business was established by acting on an observation.

Take some time to be more observant of your key customers—you can't fill an unperceived need. Some years ago, I was in a New York City subway station when I observed a young woman with a baby in a stroller. She was standing still at the top of an escalator. I assumed she wanted to go down but couldn't lift the stroller. She wasn't asking for help but it was clear she needed it. Then as I was coming up the escalator from the opposite direction, a young man appeared out of nowhere and asked if she needed help—with great relief she smiled and said, "Oh yes, would you please?" Even though there was no cry for help, he noticed her distress and came to her aid.

"Wowing" Customers

Being responsive to customers' needs, minimally, reduces or eliminates customer dissatisfaction. But don't equate the absence of customer dissatisfaction with customer satisfaction. Customer satisfaction comes from consistently meeting customers' expectations.

But we shouldn't just stop at customer satisfaction. The secret to enduring customer relationships is "wowing" the customer. We "wow" our customers by exceeding their expectations—by *anticipating* customer needs and delivering on these needs before they are even aware of them. I remember the first time I ate lunch at the famous Stage Deli in New York City. I was munching away on one of their signature sandwiches, thinking, "Boy, could I sure go for another one of their incredible pickles right about now." At that very moment, from around the corner, appeared our waiter, Norm, holding a plate with two pickles on it. I said, "How did you know that I wanted more pickles?" And I'll never forget his reply. He said, "I know what my customers want before they know what they want."

Norm was tuned in to his customers. He studied them, anticipated their needs, and delivered on them with impeccable timing. Doing the unexpected (as long as it's positive) at the right time will endear you to your customer and build customer loyalty. Loyal customers will stay with you for the long haul. Doing the unexpected may involve doing something that is uncharacteristic for you; for example, getting up for the 3 a.m. baby feeding so your wife can sleep a few extra hours, or sitting down with your husband and watching a sporting event. We can "wow" our customers by changing annoying ingrained habits and behaviors without being nagged to do so. It's important to demonstrate to our customers that we are committed to making our relationships with them as strong as possible, even if we "backslide" from time to time.

Recovery Strategies

Another way to "wow" customers is to have a great recovery strategy in place for the times we goof up. Recovery strategies are a form of sincere apology with some additional benefit attached to it. They are used frequently in business when a customer experiences less than expected quality in a product or service. Interestingly enough, a well thought out and executed recovery strategy will not only prevent the loss of a customer, but also will build a stronger and more enduring bond. A good recovery strategy follows these guidelines:

- Acknowledge that you made a mistake—and be quick about it.
- Take responsibility and be accountable—don't make excuses or try to blame someone else.

- Communicate what you're going to do about the problem and when you're going to do it.
- Compensate for your mistake by doing something for your customer that's above and beyond what they expect.
- Inform your customer what you're going to do to prevent the problem from happening again.
- Don't dwell on it for too long—learn from your mistakes, and move on.

10 Secrets to Winning Customers for Life

Although developed for business, I believe the following ten secrets to winning customers for life can be applied to our personal lives. It also serves as a nice summary of this chapter. It was sent to me by a former student who credited it to the *Better Business Bureau of Houston*. I've added my own non-business translation for each.

1. **Get to know your customers.**
   Translation: Make the time to get to know your loved ones on a deeper level. Work to understand their stated as well as unstated needs, concerns, and aspirations.
2. **Make service your number one priority.**
   Translation: Be responsive to the needs of others—be quick to offer help.
3. **Set high standards of performance.**
   Translation: Raise the bar high—set standards for yourself according to what you would expect from others.
4. **Encourage customer feedback.**
   Translation: Don't assume that everything is fine—ask for opinions from others in the spirit of continuous self-improvement.

5. **Work to exceed customer expectations.**
   Translation: Go above and beyond what is expected of you.
6. **Make your service program easy for the customer.**
   Translation: If you fall short, don't offer convoluted excuses. Be quick to apologize and offer concrete ways you can make up for your mistake.
7. **Market your customer service program.**
   Translation: Don't be timid or hold back. Be proactive in helping others. Put all your God-given gifts and talent to use.
8. **Smile and show your customers you care.**
   Translation: Be approachable and genuine when dealing with others.
9. **Support customer service throughout your life.**
   Translation: You're a Christian for life—there's no turning it on or off. You have become a changed person forever.
10. **Listen first, then respond.**
    Translation: There's a reason why God gave us two ears and one mouth. Be quick to listen (with your heart) and slow to talk.

Now you can go back and replace the word "customer" with "neighbor"!

Chapter 6 continues to build on the concept of We Power by highlighting an essential component of high-quality customer service—communication. In this next chapter, you discover effective communication techniques for building high-touch relationships in a high-tech world.

Building High-Touch Relationships in a High-Tech World

O n January 11th, 1838, Samuel Morse telegraphed the first long distance communication (over two miles) that read, "A patient waiter is no loser." By 1861, Morse's invention would connect the entire United States from coast to coast. The telegraph forever changed the way the world would communicate and exchange information. Approximately 90 years later, long-distance telephone service became available, and another 60 years or so after that, the Internet hit the world scene. Today, we can call anyone anywhere in the world *and* access the Internet from a device that's small enough to fit in the palm of our hands. Ironically, in today's world of social media and hyper-connectivity developing close personal relationships with other people is more challenging than ever. Yet, this skill is essential for harnessing We Power.

We often attribute a smartphone obsession to the younger generations, but from Millennials to Gen-Xers to Baby Boomers, we all are just as prone to technology addiction. On any given night, following dinner, Jim and Barb head to their computers. The kids, meanwhile, quickly finish homework and are then glued to their phones. Although they may be in the room at the same time, they are living in separate worlds.

This phenomenon of tech reliance can cause problems at work, as well. One CEO I coached communicated almost exclusively via text and email—even when dealing with touchy subjects. Once, when handling a crisis, I suggested that he simply walk across the hall. He followed my advice and cleared up the misunderstanding in moments, instead of going back and forth with his colleague on email for hours or even days.

This chapter provides practical tips on how to achieve a harmonious coexistence by establishing a healthy balance between hi-tech and hi-touch. Through balanced communications, we can develop stronger interpersonal relationships with our spouses, children, friends, colleagues, and neighbors.

It was a crisp Autumn Sunday afternoon—one of those days when my wife, Catherine, and I felt like being lazy. We settled into the living room, she with her reading and I intent on watching what was built up to be quite a football game (this was of course in BK era—before kids). Before long, I was deeply immersed in the game. Then, out of nowhere, there was a "whack" on my arm accompanied by the comment, "You haven't heard a word I've said have you?"

I said, "I don't know, what did you say?"

Apparently, Catherine had been trying to engage me in discussion without success. Finally, to really test whether I was listening, she announced in a loud, exasperated voice, "Scott, I'm leaving you!" to which there was still no reply, which is what precipitated the playful whack on the arm. Although we laughed about it, it reminded us how easy it is to become so absorbed or distracted with other things that it hinders the communication process.

How often do you find yourself so deeply involved in life's busyness that you fail to sense what's going on around you? A recent study conducted by Microsoft reveals that our attention span is growing increasingly short, down from 12 seconds in 2000 to eight seconds today—a full second shorter than that of a goldfish! But we can (and should) do better. The following is an excerpt from a sermon delivered by a client and friend, Rabbi David:

> We can listen better to one another. When our kids get home from school, we can listen to them about the challenges of adolescence or the joys they experienced at a rock concert. When our parents come home from work, we can listen to them about what matters most to them and how hard they have tried to improve our lives. When our parents are older, we can listen to their memories about life and cherish being present with them even when it is difficult to watch them age.
>
> When our friends are in need, we can listen to their pain and comfort them. We can listen to what people truly want to say to us, what they have to say to us.

Much has been written on how to effectively communicate. This chapter is not intended to be the definitive, comprehensive treatment on the subject. Rather, it's an attempt to share what I have found through the actual practice and observation of others, as a counselor and consultant, to be simple, yet powerful communication techniques.

Communication as a Two-Way Process

First, let's cover some communication basics. According to Webster, communication is "a process by which information is exchanged between individuals through a common system of symbols, signs, or behavior." Let's key in on an important piece of this definition—"a *process* by which information is exchanged. . . . " Indeed, communication is a process.

Communication (regardless of what form it takes) requires two components: transmitting and receiving. This seems like such a simple concept. So why then is communication cited so often as the cause of so many problems? Part of the answer is that no one really ever teaches us formally how to communicate. Instead, we learn informally as children, through the example of others. Chances are that our examples, or role models, also did not have formal training in communication and may have passed on some bad habits. These habits become ingrained in us and, unfortunately, do not change unless we make a conscious endeavor to do so.

Managing the Communication Process

You will become much more effective at building powerful relationships once you learn how to manage the communication process.

It starts with knowing *what* you want to say. Words too often become a source of misunderstanding. We all have a tendency to speak without first carefully considering what we wish to convey, the response we expect, and how the other person might receive and respond to the message. Think before you speak—and before you send a potentially upsetting text or email message. Prior to uttering a word, consider these three factors commonly taught in high school English composition classes for writing essays:

- **Audience**: Put yourself in the other person's shoes. Think about the most effective way to convey your message to that specific person. Consider how this person might misinterpret your message or misconstrue your intent.
- **Purpose**: Clarify the desired outcome. What do you hope to achieve by conveying your message? If you achieve that purpose, what is the cost or benefit to the other person?

Does your purpose align with the other person's? Can you find a way to bring your interests into better alignment?

- **Tone:** Take your emotional pulse. Are you happy, angry, suspicious, genuinely concerned, afraid, or eager? How do you want the other person to perceive your emotional state? How does the emotion conveyed in your message further or detract from your purpose? Remember, how you express yourself often has more impact than the content of your message.

Furthermore, make sure that the point you are trying to convey is not obscured with unnecessary "clutter" or information overload. A good practice is to write out what you want to say before saying it, whenever the situation allows for it. This is especially important when communicating in-person, when you don't have the opportunity to edit your message. It's also helpful when contacting someone via phone—when you are more likely to get transferred to voicemail than have the person pick up. When this happens, we usually do one of two things—either get flustered and hang up or leave an unrehearsed, incoherent message. Having a carefully edited message or at least detailed notes in writing helps to ensure that we convey the desired information.

How many times have you left an unprepared message feeling like a complete fool after you've hung up, thinking, "Oh my gosh, what did I just say?" The same can happen through email and especially texts. How many times have you hit the Send button only to wish in futility minutes later that you could un-send the message? Check and double-check your communication and make sure it conveys what you wish it to. And, as the final test, ask yourself, "How would I feel if I were the recipient of this message?" This is especially important if you are transmitting sensitive, potentially upsetting content.

Preparing the Appropriate Environment

Prior to communicating in person or over the phone, it's important to create just the right "listening" environment.

Carrying on a conversation or delivering an important message is difficult in the midst of distractions and heightened emotions. You can, and should, prepare your external environment to facilitate effective dialogue. Here are a few tips for preparing an effective listening environment.

Remove All Possible Distractions

Have you ever tried to talk to someone while their face was buried in a newspaper or their eyes glued to the TV set or a smartphone screen? It can be frustrating, to say the least. Unfortunately, distractions have become ubiquitous. At home, school, work, and nearly everywhere else, we are surrounded by people and media demanding our attention.

Regardless of who starts the conversation, take the initiative to remove the distractions. This means forwarding your phone calls if you're meeting with someone in your office. If I'm in a scheduled meeting in my office, I will never answer a ringing phone unless I am expecting an urgent call. It is disrespectful and inconsiderate to respond to an unscheduled phone interruption when you're in a scheduled meeting. How do you feel when it happens to you? At home, it means putting down your smartphone, closing your laptop, or turning off the television. I enjoy reading the daily newspaper uninterrupted, but if someone wants to talk to me when I'm reading, I make it a point to put the paper down and give the person my complete, undivided attention. You never want to send the message that an inanimate object is more important than a human being.

Don't hesitate to remind someone else either. If I'm speaking to someone who is obviously distracted, I bring it to their attention—diplomatically of course. I may say something like, "It looks as though you're busy with other things right now. Is there a better time for us to talk? What I have to discuss with you is very important, and I want to be sure that I have your complete attention."

Choose the Right Time and Place

Choose a place that's conducive to the nature of the discussion, and schedule a suitable time to meet. If you're like most people, chances are that you communicate with your important customers on-the-fly or while you or the other person or both are multi-tasking. Although that may be fine for routine communications, if you're having a serious conversation, multi-tasking significantly increases the odds of misunderstandings.

Avoid initiating a serious conversation when you're heading out the door or have a pressing issue to attend to. Don't bring up sensitive topics during family mealtimes, and never have grown-up conversations in the presence of children. Of course, serious family discussions may involve one or more children or the entire family, but such discussions should be handled in separate meetings, each in its own appropriate place and time.

If an important message can wait, schedule a time as soon as possible to have the discussion, and choose an appropriate place to meet. Early on in our relationship, Catherine and I found that we could communicate best while walking (preferably in nature) or dining at our favorite restaurant. Both locations provided a relaxed and peaceful environment enabling us to be totally present to each other. We've continued in this tradition, even though the demands on our time are far greater. If an important discussion can't wait, be creative; for example, call in to work and tell them you'll be late, cancel an appointment, or reschedule a date. Wait until you put the kids on the bus or until they are asleep.

Do whatever it takes to be *present* to the other person. If it's important enough to them to talk immediately, it should be important enough for you to rearrange your schedule and give your customer your undivided attention.

Avoid Impromptu Discussions

Sometimes our customers pop in on us unexpectedly, in person or on the phone, to discuss an issue or problem. If the matter is urgent, you probably want to drop everything and devote your full attention to listening to and responding to your customer. You may also want to address the issue immediately if it requires very little time and effort or you're not engaged in more important or pressing activities. After all, customers value responsiveness, and quick attention to minor issues keeps your to-do list from becoming unwieldy.

However, if you're already immersed in more pressing business and the discussion can wait, schedule a specific time to speak with the other person, explaining that you'd like to give them 100% of your time and attention. Businesses often set a policy of responding to customer queries within 24 to 48 hours. Most customers are fine with waiting, as long as you let them know you're on top of things and plan to get back with them within a certain amount of time.

E-Communication Tips

Communicating electronically via text messages, email, and tweets, and so on, is always tricky, because you and the other person can't see or hear one another. You don't have the benefit of non-verbal communication to express yourself or read the other person's facial expressions and body language for clues about how the person is responding to your message. Nor do you have the opportunity to immediately correct yourself to clarify your message if you sense a misunderstanding. In this section, I provide some guidance on how to communicate more effectively via electronic channels.

Most importantly, never message when you're:

- Angry, frustrated, or afraid (frustration and fear often quickly turn to anger)

- Tired
- Rushed
- Impaired

When dealing with an emotional or complex issue, compose your message and then, instead of sending it immediately, save the draft. Review it later when you've calmed down and are clear-headed. If possible, have a friend or colleague review it. Be clear on what you intend to communicate and how you want your message to register with the person on the receiving end.

Keep in mind that e-communication isn't always the most effective means of communication. Meeting in person, over the phone, or via video-conferencing is often better when dealing with sensitive or pressing issues or when you need to agree on details, such as a date, time, and place to meet. A 60-second phone call can save a lot of texting or emailing back and forth.

Communication Skills

"Know this, my beloved brothers: let every person be quick to hear, slow to speak, slow to anger; for the anger of man does not produce the righteousness of God" (James 1:19–20 ESV).

Communication is an interactive, often repetitive process of receiving, interpreting, and sending messages—not necessarily in that order. To engage in productive dialogue, I encourage you to develop what I deem are the three most important communication skills:

- Managing disagreement
- Providing feedback
- Empathetic listening

Empathetic Listening

The Chinese characters that make up the verb "to listen" tell us something significant about this skill as they contain the words "heart," "undivided attention," "ear," and "eyes."

Heart

Empathetic listening begins with the *heart*. It involves compassionately sharing in the humanity of another. We can be "present" to another person when we truly care about them and put their needs in front of our own, no matter what the issue. To listen with your heart is to step mind, body, and soul into another's laughter, pain, joy, and sorrow.

Undivided Attention

Empathetic listening requires that you give another your *undivided attention* regardless of what's going on around you.

Many years ago, I attended a conference that featured as its keynote speaker, Stephen Covey, best-selling author of *The 7 Habits of Highly Effective People*. After his speech, a long, winding line formed for a book signing, and it was moving painfully slowly. After a while, I started to get impatient and, frankly, somewhat annoyed. I started thinking, "What's taking so long? What's he doing up there?" Eventually, my turn came, and it was then that I discovered the reason for the delay. The minute I introduced myself, his eyes locked into mine. It was as though we were the only two people in the room.

Never mind that we were in a crowded, noisy, smoke-filled convention hall. We had a delightful, unhurried conversation—much to the chagrin of the many others still waiting in line! That encounter had a lasting impression on me.

Someone once told me that the secret to giving someone your undivided attention is to tell yourself that "the person I'm talking to is the most important person in the world." Another way to give someone your undivided attention is to avoid the temptation of finishing their thoughts before they've had a chance to speak or fully express themselves. This can be accomplished by pressing your tongue up against the roof of your mouth—the equivalent of "holding your tongue" (but far less messy!). Instead of thinking about what you'll say next, focus exclusively on understanding what the other person is saying.

Ears

Empathetic listening requires the use of your natural equipment—namely your *ears*. Did you know that you have an ear in your heart? Well, sort of. If you look closely at the word "heart", you'll see that it contains the word "ear." As mentioned in the previous chapter, the reason God gave us two ears and one mouth is so we can listen twice as much as we talk.

Eyes

Empathetic listening requires making good use of your *eyes*. Did you ever try to carry on a conversation with someone whose eyes were darting around? It immediately sends a signal that "I'm not really listening."

Just yesterday, I stepped into OR stopped by a telecommunications outlet to look into a new plan for my cell phone. I approached the customer service counter and stood in front of the representative who was seated behind a desk. Without even looking up at me he asked, "What can I do for you?" As I started to speak, I realized he was still looking down, preoccupied.

After I described what I was looking for, he mumbled, "You need to see Matt," and gestured to a young man across the aisle. Not once did he look at me. I decided to try one of their competitors and walked out of the store disappointed. Making good eye contact tells the other person that they're important and that you care about them and their needs.

Some people are good at faking it. They pretend to be listening by making occasional eye contact and throwing in a nod of the head and a frequent "uh huh." Empathetic listening is not just hearing what people are saying. It's actively listening to what they're saying.

The best way to demonstrate active listening is to *clarify* and *confirm* what you're hearing. *Clarifying* is making sure you understand what you heard by seeking additional information. *Confirming* typically involves expressing your understanding of what you heard. Confirmation occurs when the two parties believe they have reached a mutual understanding of what transpired during the discussion, including any agreements, decisions, and items tabled for future discussion. Effective questioning techniques can facilitate the clarification and confirmation process.

Open- vs. Close-Ended Questioning

When clarifying, be mindful of *how* you ask questions. A *close-ended question* usually elicits a yes/no, or some other form of short response; for example, "Did you have fun at the party?" It provides little information or insight and tends to limit the discussion. Close-ended questions can also take on the tone of an interrogation and be a turn-off to the other person.

Although close-ended questions can certainly be useful, make liberal use of open-ended questioning, which invites dialogue. For instance, instead of asking, "Did you have fun at the party?" you could try, "Tell me about the party." I've found this to be especially useful when talking to my children. Ask any child, "How was school today?" and you'll generally receive a one-word response: "Okay." I've learned to rephrase to an open-ended question which always gets a better response: "Tell me about school today." or "Tell me at least one thing you learned about in school today."

Try your best to avoid using the word "why." It can quickly shut down the communication process by putting the other person on the defensive: "Why did you do that?" "Why are you upset with me?" Whenever possible, replace the word "why" with "what"; for example, "What is it that has made you so upset with me?"

Continue to clarify during the discussion by repeating what you think you're hearing and checking for accuracy; for example, to request clarification, you may say something like, "So let me see if I understand what you're saying . . ." followed by your *interpretation* of what you heard in your own words. Parroting the same words back to the sender does not demonstrate that you understand the *meaning* of what they said.

The clarification process continues with further questioning until final confirmation that occurs when the transmitter is confident that the receiver has heard and understood the message.

Defining Terms

Sometimes, thinking that we have confirmation, we act only to find out later that our understanding was incorrect. The cause for such misunderstanding is often due to a lack of agreement over the definitions of key words and phrases. The same word may have multiple meanings depending on the individual. We can avoid problems downstream if we take the time to make sure we have the same understanding of the terminology we use.

I'm sure you've run across this with your teen-aged children when, on a Friday night, they say, "I'm going out with some friends. I won't be home too late." These two simple sentences contain at least three terms with vague meanings that are calling out for clarification. Can you spot them? They are, "out," "friends," and "not too late." As a concerned parent, you want to know just *where* "out" is, *which* "friends," and *how* "late." You don't want to make any assumptions—your interpretations may be very different from your teenager's. Using questioning techniques, probe more to discover the exact meaning, as in the following example. I refer to the details in the right column as "operational definitions," because they specify the term's practical or concrete meaning.

Word (or Term)	Operational Definition
"Out"	The movies (at the local theater)
"Friends"	Steve, Mark, Jack
"Not too late"	Home 11:30 p.m.

Generally speaking, as parents we tend to do a better job operationally defining words with our children than we do with other adults. As adults, we often neglect this important step. We think that just because we're talking, we're communicating. Talking is only the first step and a good one at that. But unless we reach an understanding, talking is nothing more than a volley of words or useless chatter. Communication with significant others is an intimate exchange resulting in deeper understanding, greater commitment, and enduring bonds. If your spouse informs you that the two of you don't spend enough time together, take the time and energy to discover what "enough" means and what "time together" means. You may say something like, "Ideally, how much time do you think we should spend together each week?" and "What do you envision when you think about us spending time together?"

Two people can spend hours in the same room together and never speak to each other. Recently, while dining alone at an elegant restaurant in New York, a couple was ushered in and seated directly in front of me. Immediately after they were seated, the man accompanying the woman received a call on his cell phone. He chatted through cocktails, appetizers, and halfway into the main course, while his dinner companion looked on. Although she tried not to look annoyed, it was apparent that she was seething. They sat at the same table together, but they didn't exactly spend quality time together. Take the time to define the meaning of words and terms used during important discussions with your customers—it's well worth the effort.

Managing Disagreement

Some people believe that disagreement in a relationship is a bad thing. But actually, if dealt with properly, disagreement can serve to enhance and strengthen a relationship. Not all communications go smoothly. Sometimes we find ourselves at odds with another person—a difference of opinion. It may seem that the best approach is to avoid the issue and the accompanying quarrel altogether. But that doesn't solve anything, and unresolved issues can fester and build up causing more serious relationship issues later.

Here's an easy-to-follow three-step process that will help you navigate through disagreement and conflict:

1. Define the difference.
2. Discuss options.
3. Bring to closure.

Step 1: Define the Difference

The first step to managing a disagreement is to clarify each other's position. Some people are from the "shoot first, ask questions later" school of thought. That is, they form their own opinions and express them without even attempting to understand the other person's point of view. Instead, let the other person speak first and express their viewpoint. Using empathetic listening, try to find out what their issues are and what's most important to them. Clarify and confirm your understanding, then state your position. Now at least you know where you both stand and why. Keep the dialogue objective by focusing on the issues—don't make it personal. This approach will help you pinpoint not only the areas of disagreement, but also areas of agreement—common ground, which is fertile ground for productive dialogue.

Here's an example:

Person A: "What is it about my working late that upsets you so much?"

Person B: "We don't ever have a chance to talk anymore. There's a lot that goes on every day, and I need to share things with you."

Person A: "But if I don't work late, things pile up, and then I get way behind. It's important to me that I do a good job. You know that I'm the next in line for a promotion to VP. The extra money will come in handy. Isn't that important to you?"

Person B: "Of course it is, but it's important to me that we don't drift apart."

The differences are clear: Person A is focused on doing quality work, getting promoted, and earning more money for the family. Person B wants more quality time as a couple. Knowing their differences, they are ready to explore options.

Step 2: Discuss Options

Both individuals have made valid points. Although they haven't resolved the disagreement, at least they have an understanding and a greater appreciation of one another's view. They are now ready to brainstorm and discuss options for solving the problem, which happens to be a mutual problem.

When you and your customer reach Step 2, be prepared to brainstorm. Listen to one another's ideas and evaluate them based what's best overall—not what's best for me or what's best for you, but what's best for us? What's best for the family? What's best for the community? Ideally, your creative synergy arrives at a perfect solution that's a win-win for both of you with little or no sacrifice required of either party. However, in most cases, you'll probably need to engage in some give and take in order to reach a consensus. This could involve compromise or even agreeing to disagree on some points. Ultimately, you want to move in the direction of a mutually satisfactory solution.

Step 3: Bring to Closure

Once an optimal solution has been arrived at, bring closure to the discussion by clarifying and finally confirming what you've agreed to. Monitor the results—things don't always go as planned. Be prepared to make adjustments to the plan or replace it with plan B or C if necessary. Don't assume that your initial plan will proceed without a hitch, and don't hesitate to acknowledge when a plan has failed and requires a change in direction. Maintain focus on the goal, and be persistent in achieving it.

Providing Feedback

"Let your speech always be gracious, seasoned with salt, so that you may know how you ought to answer each person" (Colossians 4:6 ESV).

Each of us is equipped with an amazing neural feedback system that we normally take for granted. The simple action of crossing a street engages all sorts of sensory and neurological messaging systems that enable us to carefully plot, time, and navigate our course. Yet, when we attempt to resolve differences with others, or we try to work with others toward a common goal, we often forget the importance of feedback in coordinating our efforts.

When you're resolving disagreements or solving problems together with your customers, feedback is crucial to your success. In the following sections, I discuss the two types of feedback, *positive* and *corrective*.

Positive Feedback

We use positive feedback when we want to reinforce certain behaviors in other people. If given in the proper manner, it increases the likelihood that the desired behavior will repeat itself. Positive feedback is more than just an "atta boy," which is far too general. Instead of merely cheering on the other person, I recommend delivering positive feedback via the following two-step process:

1. Give a specific example.
2. Describe the benefit or result.

Let the person know exactly what it was that they did and why it was helpful to you; for example, you may say something like, "Hey Alyson, thanks for helping me with my job search yesterday. I especially appreciate that you reviewed my resume. Your suggestions gave it a more professional look, and, as a result, I think I have a better chance of landing interviews."

Those are the "do's." Giving positive feedback also comes with a few don'ts:

- Don't be patronizing. Be genuine and sincere in expressing your gratitude.
- Don't overdo it. Some people are lavish with their praise, which makes people feel good. But good feelings are temporary—being selective will have a specific effect on the individual leading to lasting behavioral change.
- Don't wait too long. Your feedback will have greater impact and meaning if given in a timely manner.
- Don't be embarrassed. Some people are uncomfortable giving positive feedback, but if you let that stop you, you miss an opportunity to provide intrinsic reward to a deserving person.

Corrective Feedback

Sometimes people fall short of our expectations, disappointing us. In these cases, corrective feedback is necessary. This involves more than simply saying, "Hey, you screwed up, and I'm upset." What you want to accomplish with corrective feedback is positive behavioral change. It's not a reprimand. Rather, it's a way to point out a mistake, error, lapse in judgment, etc. without damaging your relationship with the other person. Corrective feedback will decrease the likelihood that an undesirable behavior or action will repeat itself.

As with positive feedback, corrective feedback is most effective when delivered properly. I recommend the following three-step process:

1. Accentuate the positive.
2. Express your concern.
3. End on a positive note.

Begin by calling attention to any positive aspects of the behavior. Always assume that the intent was pure. Many years ago, my kids surprised me for Father's Day with breakfast in bed. After enjoying my breakfast, I walked into the kitchen, and it looked like a tornado ripped through it. I was faced with somewhat of a dilemma—do I say something or just keep my mouth shut? I thought, "If I say something I'll hurt their feelings. If I don't say something, they won't learn. . . ."

Using the three-step process, I accentuated the positive by telling them how surprised and pleased I was at their thoughtfulness. I also commented on how delicious breakfast was. Next, which is always the difficult part, I gently expressed my concern. I pointed out that unless things were put away, they could spoil or attract bugs. I also reminded them that it's a good practice, in general, to clean up after ourselves.

I certainly didn't want them to think that they could leave the mess for mom to clean up. Then the three of us cleaned the place up. Since then, on the occasions when they've made breakfast, they've been sure to pick up afterwards. After you express your concern, finish the conversation on a positive note by reminding them of the merit of their action. For instance, you might say, "I really appreciate the effort you put into making breakfast for me. It was very thoughtful of you."

Here are some additional tips to keep in mind when giving corrective feedback:

- Keep negative emotions in check. You may have every right to be angry, but don't let it get the best of you. Showing that you're upset is okay as long as you don't lash out at the other person.
- Avoid "trapdoor" words like "but" and "however" when transitioning (for example, "You're a really nice person, *but.* . . .") Simply replace the "but" or "however" with a pause.
- Don't sugarcoat your message. If you focus too much on the positive, your concern may go unnoticed.
- Don't be afraid. Giving corrective feedback is uncomfortable, but if we don't do it, we're not helping others learn and grow. Former GE CEO, Jack Welch, in a speech at Fairfield University, referred to this as his "tough love" approach. He believed, as I do, that sometimes we have to be brutally honest with people. They may not like to hear it at first, but if done with love and compassion, they'll respect us for it.
- Put yourself in the recipient's shoes. Everybody reacts in different ways to corrective feedback. Try to match your style to theirs. Some people prefer a more direct approach, without any beating around the bush. Others may be very sensitive and require a gentler, more indirect approach. Know who you're dealing with, and adjust your style accordingly.
- Be discrete: "Praise in public, and criticize (correct) in private." Praise in public, especially when you want others to learn from (and model) similar behaviors. When criticizing or correcting, do it privately to avoid public shaming, which can be devastating to the person on the receiving end. The aim is to build up and empower—not drag down.

Reflect on the words of Paul: "Let no corrupting talk come out of your mouths, but only such as is good for building up, as fits the occasion, that it may give grace to those who hear" (Ephesians 4:29 ESV).

Jesus admonishes us to love one another. I believe that the manner in which we communicate is a very important way to demonstrate our love for others. At the end of the classic movie, *The Wizard of Oz*, the Wizard tells the Tin Man, who is in search of a heart, to "remember my friend that a man's heart is not judged by how much he loves, but how much he is loved by others." Building rapport with others will help to ensure loving, enduring relationships!

PART 3

Thee Power

Thee Power is the ultimate power. It represents our deep, direct connection to God. We can make this connection in many different ways, but primarily through prayer, meditation, and contemplation. Supplemental methods include attending religious services, Bible study, and reading scripture and inspirational books. This is an inward power for "The Kingdom of God is within."

Thee Power involves continual thoughtful introspection and communication with God—an acknowledgement of God and a sincere and active interest in getting to know Him better. This inward power employs the mind, heart, and soul toward closer engagement with God.

In this Part, you discover

- What it means to be a Christian
- Practical ways for getting to know God
- How faith changes lives

CHAPTER 7

What It Means To Be a Christian

Mahatma Gandhi was asked once, "Why don't you become a Christian? You already do all or most of the things Jesus said we should do." Gandhi replied, "I might become a Christian if ever I should see one."

I believe that the biggest enemies of Christianity in its truest form are people masquerading as Christians. They are Christian in name only, while their actual behavior is antithetical to what the religion teaches. Unfortunately, the problem starts with the leadership of various Christian denominations, who have been convicted of corruption and scandal after scandal in recent years. Even though less than one percent of clergy are involved in such misdeeds, still the horror of their actions and the subsequent denial by Church leadership have caused many to leave the faith.

Others at fault are extremists—so-called Christians who think nothing of blowing up abortion clinics or killing doctors. Violence, racism, and prejudice have no place in Christianity. Even though such "believers" are few, they grab the majority of headlines. Who on earth would want to be a member of that "club"?

This chapter explores misinterpretations and misconceptions about Christianity and Christians, while illuminating the true meaning of the faith, and its corresponding behavior and actions.

Some people think that a Christian is one who does good deeds for others and tries to live an honorable life. Actually, that can be said of any faith or non-faith for that matter. Think about what the word "Christian" really means. We are not only followers of Christ and his tenets but *partisans*. To be partisan is to take sides. Yes, we are called to side with Christ versus the world and all its empty promises. This means asking Him to come into our lives—in a sense, surrendering ourselves to him. It means we strive to live up to the ideals Jesus set, taught, and modeled for us. It means acknowledging with sincere sorrow when we have failed to live up to His standards (when we have sinned) and accepting His forgiving grace.

My local paper features a column by the Reverend Billy Graham entitled, "My Answer." In a recent edition, the following question was posed: "I am trying to decide which religion I want to follow. How did you decide that you wanted to be a Christian? I don't have any religion background, but now that I'm out of college I've decided I need to start thinking about it." It was signed "R.W." Reverend Graham replied as follows:

> Dear R.W., I am grateful for my parents' example of faith in Christ and for their commitment to take me to church and teach me about the Bible. No doubt God used these to prepare me to make my own commitment to Christ as a teenager. But I became a Christian not because I grew up in a Christian family or went to church, but because I sensed a need in my heart to have my sins forgiven and to know God personally. I realized later that God had put that desire within me—and I believe he is doing the same in your life. Within everyone of us is what has been called "a God-shaped vacuum"—a spiritual emptiness in our souls only God can fill. My prayer is that you won't try to fill it with anything less than the living God. This is why I urge you to turn to Jesus Christ, for he was

God in human flesh, sent from Heaven to open the way to God. Only one thing separates us from God, and that is our sin—and we cannot erase our own sins by our own efforts. But by his death on the cross, Christ became the final sacrifice for our sins. Ask God to help you discover from the Bible who Jesus is and what he has done for you—and then give your life to him.

Reverend Graham's response tells us much about what Christianity is all about and what it means to be a Christian. In this chapter, I touch on the key aspects of what it means to be a Christian and explain each as concisely and clearly as possible:

- God the Father and Creator of All
- Original sin
- The devil/hell
- God's promise
- Jesus
  - Birth
  - Life
  - Death
  - Resurrection
- The Holy Spirit
- Heaven and eternal life

Now, let's take a closer look at each.

God the Father and Creator of All

Before wading into this topic, I must point out that much debate swirls around whether we should interpret the Bible literally or allegorically. For instance, Genesis tells us that God created the universe and everything in it in six days. He rested on the seventh. A literal interpretation indicates that these were 24-hour days. However, those who view the creation story allegorically maintain that creation may have occurred over a long period of time. I believe that nearly all of the Bible is historically accurate. Archaeologists have found plenty of evidence to support the contents of both the Old and New Testaments and seem to dig up more evidence with each passing year. Many people struggle with the Biblical account of creation and question its scientific accuracy. I suggest not getting too caught up on that which can be a stumbling block. I consider it to be an accurate depiction of God as Creator and humans as being separated from God due to our inherent human nature. I believe the messages and lessons gleaned from scripture are intended to enable us to better understand the Creator and to fully achieve our incredible human potential as God intended.

Moving on, most people are well familiar with the story of creation detailed in the book of Genesis ("Genesis" means "origin"). If you haven't read Genesis yet, I highly recommend it. In the meantime, I'll share some takeaways. First, we learn that God is responsible for the creation of the universe—heaven and earth and all that is contained in it. As Christians, we believe that God always was, is, and ever shall be. In Revelation 21:6, we learn that God is the "Alpha" and the "Omega"—the beginning and the end. Alpha is the first letter in the Greek alphabet and Omega is the last. I understand that this is difficult for many to grasp, giving us cause to wonder "Where did God come from?" The philosophers have grappled with this question throughout the ages. As Christians, we accept the answer presented in the Bible on faith. God also created human beings *in His image*. Before going further, this is an important point. The Bible does not specify exactly what this means, but minimally we can infer that *all* human beings have been created in His image; hence, we all have inherent value and dignity—regardless of our position in life. When Jesus gave us The Lord's Prayer, He begins with the words, "Our

Father." This also suggests an inclusiveness versus some kind of exclusive club reserved for a select few. That God created all people in His image implies that we must respect all human life and at every stage—from womb to tomb.

Continuing with the creation story, we're told that God made human beings male and female, "blessed them, and said, 'Have many children, so that your descendants will live all over the earth and bring it under control. I am putting you in charge of the fish, the birds, and all the wild animals'" (Genesis 1:27–29 GNT). We are instructed not only to populate the earth, but also to preserve and manage the amazing resources God has provided. We are to be good stewards of God's creation.

Original Sin

As you know, it all started in The Garden of Eden. God placed man in the garden to tend to it and allowed him to eat any of the fruit produced with one exception: Under no circumstances should he eat the fruit of the tree that gives knowledge of what is good and what is bad. If he disobeys God and eats from that particular tree, he will die the same day. Later, God removes a rib from the sleeping man and creates woman (and at this point, we're not yet aware of their names).

The woman encounters a snake, which the Bible describes as the most cunning animal that the Lord had made. The snake convinces the woman that she should eat of the fruit because it would make her "like God," knowing what is good and what is evil. So she took some of the fruit and ate it and then gave some to her husband.

When God found out, he punished the snake and the man and woman. The snake was cursed to crawl on its belly, eating dust, and to be forever at war with the woman and her offspring. Regarding the woman, God told her He would increase her trouble in pregnancy and her pain in giving birth. As for the man, he would have to work hard all his life, toiling in the ground and eventually returning to it—"dust to dust."

We learn of their names toward the end of the garden scene— Adam (which in Hebrew means "humankind") and Eve. Adam gives Eve that name because she is the mother of all human beings. Finally, God banishes them from the Garden of Eden. Adam and Eve's original sin, their disobedience of God's command, ensured that the entire human race would be like God, being able to tell good from evil, but resulted in the entire human race being banished from the Garden of Eden and separated from God and the Tree of Life. Sin and death, therefore, would be inevitably passed down from generation to generation. This is a critical event for Christians as it sets the stage for the coming of the Messiah, our Savior, Jesus Christ.

The Devil/Hell

I am amazed at the number of Christians I encounter who don't believe in the devil and hell. Often the reasoning goes something like this, "Why would a loving, just God banish anybody to an eternity of hell?" Further stoking the flames of disbelief are books and articles debunking the whole idea of a fiery inferno run by a garish red beast with horns and long tail carrying a pitchfork.

Some thinkers simply question the usefulness of the concept. For instance, a recent article in *The Wall Street Journal* by Dr. Scott Bruce, professor of history at Fordham University, was entitled, "Do We Still Need to Believe in Hell?" At the closing of the article, Dr. Bruce writes:

> Has Hell outlived its usefulness in modern society? Probably not. The doctrine still serves Christianity as a frightening deterrent to sinful behavior. We still hope that wicked people and corrupt leaders will get their just deserts in the world to

come. In some distant, better future, the foreclosure of Hell will be an important step in the matu-
ration of human communities that can mete out
justice on their own, without supernatural aid.

I realize that Dr. Bruce is writing as a historian and not as
a theologian. His cynical view is shared by many agnostics and
atheists, as well as some so-called Christians. He suggests that
hell is a fear-driven invention designed to keep us all on the
straight and narrow.

The notion of the devil and his existence is referred to numerous times in the Bible. Many believe that the snake, or serpent,
in the Garden of Eden was actually the devil. This is reinforced
in Ezekiel, which references a king that was once an example of
perfection. In the passage, the Lord says:

> How wise and handsome you were! You lived
> in Eden, the garden of God. . . . Your conduct
> was perfect from the day you were created until
> you began to do evil. You were busy buying and
> selling, and this led you to violence and sin. So
> I forced you to leave my holy mountain, and the
> angel who guarded you drove you away from the
> sparkling gems. You were proud of being hand-
> some, and your fame made you look like a fool.
> Because of this I hurled you to the ground and left
> you as a warning to other kings (Ezekiel 28:15–18
> GNT).

The devil makes numerous appearances in the New Testament
as well. For example, the Gospel of Matthew shares the story of
the temptation of Jesus by the devil right before Jesus begins
his public ministry. Beginning at Chapter 4:1, Matthew writes,
"Then the Spirit led Jesus into the desert to be tempted by the

devil." The devil first tempts a famished Jesus to turn stones into bread to satisfy his hunger. Jesus refuses, quoting scripture, "Man cannot live on bread alone but needs every word that God speaks." Then the Devil takes Jesus to the highest point in the Holy City of Jerusalem. He tells Jesus to throw himself down. If He's truly God's son, He will be unharmed. Jesus replies by once again quoting scripture, "Do not put the Lord God to the test." Finally, the devil takes Jesus to a high mountain, showing Him all the kingdoms of the world and their greatness. He tells Jesus that all could be His if only He kneels down and worships him. Of course, Jesus rebukes the devil. "Go away Satan! For the scripture says, 'Worship the Lord your God and serve only Him.' Then the devil left Jesus, and angels came and helped Him."

Let me be very clear here: *You cannot call yourself a Christian and at the same time deny the existence of evil, sin, and its consequences.* As St. Paul writes in his letter to the Romans, "The wages of sin is death; but the gift of God is eternal life through Jesus Christ our Lord" (Romans 6:23 NLT).

The Devil's Job
The devil and his minions have one job and one job only—to steal souls. We must be on our guard at all times and stay strong because he is a cunning and ruthless adversary:

> Finally, build up your strength in union with the Lord and by means of his mighty power. Put on all the armor that God gives you, so that you will be able to stand up against the devil's evil tricks. For we are not fighting against human beings but against the wicked spiritual forces in the heavenly world, the rulers, authorities, and cosmic powers of this dark age (Ephesians 6:10–12 GNT).

Further, St. Peter warns us:

> Be alert, be on watch! Your enemy, the devil,
> roams around like a roaring lion looking for some-
> one to devour. Be firm in your faith and resist
> him, because you know that your fellow believers
> in all the world are going through the same kind
> of sufferings (1 Peter 5:8–9 GNT).

I believe the devil works in two distinct ways, similar to a Jekyll and Hyde as portrayed in the Robert Louis Stevenson's classic, *The Strange Case of Dr. Jekyll and Mr. Hyde*. The story is about one man with two very distinct personalities—Jekyll who is friendly and approachable, and Hyde, who is a hideous monster. When the devil is in his Hyde mode, the world experiences violence, ruthlessness, bloodshed, and death. An example in the twentieth century was the Holocaust, which was clearly perpetrated by the devil using Hitler as his tool. In the twenty-first century, we experienced another vivid example of the devil at work: 9/11 and other acts of terror, bombings, executions, school shootings, the indiscriminate killing of innocent people attending an outdoor concert in Las Vegas, and so on. They all have the markings of evil actively at work, bringing nothing but death and destruction.

A year after the Las Vegas massacre, experts still were unable to explain the motive for why a seemingly well-adjusted man opened fire on a crowd killing 58 people and wounding 489 others. We apply Band-Aid solutions such as gun control or increasing assistance for those with mental health problems. We seem to be unable to recognize that evil is what's really at work. We've pushed God to the side leaving a vacuum filled by the devil.

In Jekyll mode, the Devil works in a very subtle, seductive manner, lulling his subjects into complacent acquiescence. Back in the 1960s, Rod Serling hosted a great science fiction series called *The Twilight Zone*. One episode entitled, "Nothing in the Dark," featured an elderly woman played by Gladys Cooper. As an old woman she is petrified of death and decides to barricade herself in her basement so that when death would come calling, he wouldn't be able to enter. Later in the evening, she hears the sound of gunfire. From a tiny window, she sees a police officer lying on the ground with a bullet wound. He cries out to her for help but she's suspicious—she thinks she's being tricked. She responds to his pleas for help saying, "I know who you are, I know *what* you are."

The seriously wounded officer continues to plead with her to let him in and help him. Still skeptical, she catches a glimpse of the officer who happens to be played by a very handsome, young Robert Redford. She thinks that he couldn't possibly be Mr. Death. She lets him in and dresses his wound. His charm, good looks, and affable nature are seductive. Over time, as she nurses him back to health, she falls in love with him. Near the end of the episode, she turns from him to get some tea. When she looks in the mirror, she sees the bed he's lying on but no reflection of him in the mirror. When she turns around to look, he's there.

In the final scene, the handsome officer takes on the appearance of Mr. Death, faceless and wearing a black hooded robe. He takes the old woman by the arm, who has been charmed into fearlessness, and escorts her out. This is the devil's favorite way to steal souls. He charms and flatters and slowly changes the way his victims think. He infiltrates individuals, families, institutions, and even entire countries, gradually winning them over to his point of view.

If I Were the Devil . . .

The late radio broadcaster, Paul Harvey, who clearly understood the devil's cunning nature shared the following with his audience:

> If I were the devil . . .
> I would gain control of the most powerful nation in the world;

I would delude their minds into thinking they had come from man's effort, instead of God's blessing;

I would promote an attitude of loving things and using people, instead of the other way around;

I would dupe entire states into relying on gambling for their revenue;

I would convince people that character is not an issue when it comes to leadership;

I would make it legal to take the life of unborn babies;

I would make it socially acceptable to take one's own life, and invent machines to make it convenient;

I would cheapen human life as much as possible so that the life of animals are valued more than human beings;

I would take God out of the schools, where even the mention of His name was grounds for a lawsuit;

I would come up with drugs that sedate the mind and target the young, and I would get sports heroes to advertise them;

I would get control of the media, so that every night I could pollute the mind of every family member for my agenda;

I would attack the family, the backbone of any nation;

I would make divorce acceptable and easy, even fashionable. If the family crumbles, so does the nation;

I would compel people to express their most depraved fantasies on canvas and movie screens, and I would call it art;

I would convince the world that people are born homosexuals and that their lifestyles should be accepted and marveled;

I would persuade people that the Church is irrelevant and out of date, and the Bible is for the naïve;

I would dull the minds of Christians, and make them believe that prayer is not important, and that faithfulness and obedience are optional;

I guess I would leave things much the way they are.

That broadcast took place a few decades ago; since then, we now allow gay marriage, and many states have legalized marijuana for recreational purposes. Assisted suicide is now legal in many countries around the world, as well as a number of states in the U.S. Clearly, social norms are changing. Using gay marriage as an example, many supporters believe that two people in love should not be denied the right to marry. I understand that thinking. Over the years, I have known many gay people who were in committed relationships—people I have worked with, clients, and friends. As a Christian, I treat everyone with respect regardless of race, creed, sexual preference, and so on. That said, though legal today, I do not condone gay marriage, just as I do not condone adultery, polygamy, having children out of wedlock, and so on.

The Bible is very clear on this—marriage is a sacred institution between one man and one woman: "That is why a man leaves his father and mother and is united with his wife, and they become one" (Genesis 2:24 GNT). But the devil convinces well-intentioned people that those unsupportive of sinful behavior are intolerant and hateful. Being tolerant should not require that the committed Christian be accepting of all behaviors. Jesus made it clear that we should not judge, but at the same time tells us we should be able to recognize sin and avoid it at all costs. As the old saying goes, "love the sinner, hate the sin." And we're all sinners. When we normalize deviant behavior that contradicts scripture, we make sin unrecognizable. In doing so, we place our soul in jeopardy. That's exactly what the devil hopes for.

God's Promises

Fortunately, regardless of what hardships and problems we encounter in life, God promises us that if we stay faithful, we will prevail against the forces of evil. But can we trust that God will keep His promises? As you peruse the Bible, you'll read many accounts of God's promises. Though too numerous to list them all, two are packed with power and filled with hope.

One of the first promises God makes is to Noah. God guides Noah, his family, and the animals through the flood while all the rest of humanity is swept away. One of Noah's first acts after the waters subside is to make an altar to God and offer a sacrifice to the Lord. This act of worship and thanksgiving pleases God, who blesses Noah and his sons, telling them to have many children in order to populate the earth. Then, God makes a binding pronouncement:

> With these words, I make my covenant with you: I promise that never again will all living beings be destroyed by a flood; never again will a flood destroy the earth. As a sign of this everlasting covenant which I am making with you and with all living beings, I am putting my bow in the clouds. It will be the sign of my covenant to the world. Whenever I cover the sky with clouds the rainbow appears, I will remember my promise to you and to all the animals that a flood will never again destroy all living beings. When the rainbow

appears in the clouds, I will see it and remember the everlasting covenant between me and all living beings on earth. That is the sign of the promise which I am making to all living beings (Genesis 9:11–17 GNT).

Throughout the Bible, just as with Noah, God shows favor to those who obey his commandments and show proper respect by praising and worshipping him. That doesn't mean He will always spare us from heartache and sorrow. But it does mean that He will see us through our darkest moments if only we place our trust in Him:

The Lord will make you go through hard times, but He Himself will be there to teach you, and you will not have to search for Him anymore. If you wander off the road to the right or left, you will hear His voice behind you saying, "Here is the road. Follow it" (Isaiah 30:20–21 GNT).

Many years ago a friend, Linda, lost her son to suicide. She and her husband were devastated. They were devout Christians and never asked God why something like this would happen. One day while driving to work, she cried out in anguish to God, "Please Lord, just give me a sign that my son is okay!" Moments after that, a rainbow appeared in the sky. Oddly, it had not been raining. In fact, it was a mostly sunny day. I realize that the cynic or skeptic would say it was sheer coincidence, but Linda took that as a clear sign that her son was with God and in good hands. A wave of peace passed through her. As she was telling me this, the following passage came to mind: "And the peace of God, which passeth all understanding, shall keep your hearts and minds through Christ Jesus" (Philippians 4:7 KJV).

Of course, the second and *greatest* promise God made to all humankind was that he would send a Savior, or Messiah, the Lamb of God who takes away the sins of the world. And why did God send his only begotten son? According to John 3:16, "For God so loved the world that He gave His only-begotten Son, so that whoever believes in Him should not perish, but have everlasting life." This is a nice lead into what we as Christians believe about the life, death, and resurrection of Jesus Christ.

Jesus Christ

In the first book of the Bible, God banishes Adam and Eve and their descendants from the Garden of Eden, preventing them access to the Tree of Life. But later in the Old Testament, our forgiving God provides a path to redemption and to eternal life. In Isaiah, God promises that a Messiah will come to free us from the bondage of sin:

> A child is born to us! A son is given to us! And He will be our ruler. He will be called, Wonderful Counselor, Mighty God, Eternal Father, and Prince of Peace. His royal power will continue to grow; His kingdom will always be at peace. He will rule as King David's successor, basing His power on right and justice, from now until the end of time. The Lord Almighty is determined to do all this (Isaiah: 9:6–7 GNT).

Jesus' Birth

The story of Jesus' birth is well-known, so I don't feel a need to retell the Christmas Story. Rather, I think it worthwhile to meditate on some important aspects of Jesus' birth and how they inform us as Christians.

Let's start with Mary. Scholars estimate that she was approximately 14 years old at the time of her betrothal. This may seem young, but back in the first century, most women were not expected to live past their 40s. Marriage was typically arranged and negotiated by the parents of the groom and bride. It involved the transfer of land as part of the bride's dowry in exchange for currency—in the event that the husband dies, the wife would have the means to support herself and her children. This marriage contract meant that the two families would essentially be kin. In today's terms, they all had skin in the game.

As had been prophesied, Mary, a virgin, would conceive a son—the Messiah, or the "anointed one." Imagine how you would react if you were her fiancée or her parents and you learned that your wife-to-be or your daughter, a virgin, was pregnant? Today, the consequences would be minimal. After all, it's the twenty-first century! But in Mary's time, a woman caught pregnant out of wedlock would be severely punished, if not stoned to death. It would also bring great shame to her family—it was her father's and her brothers' responsibility to protect her chastity. In those times, the betrothed were not allowed to be left alone unattended. Some mistakenly believe that Joseph and Mary were already married when their families reached an agreement that they would be married. The actual wedding would take place at some point following.

Back to Mary. She's all alone when the angel Gabriel appears to her with the incredible news that God has chosen her to bring Jesus into the world. At first, Mary is troubled; after all, she couldn't possibly be pregnant since she did not have relations with a man. Gabriel responds to her, "The Holy Spirit shall come upon you and the power of the Most High shall overshadow you; therefore that holy Offspring will be called the Son of God" (Luke 1:35 AKJV).

This represents a pivotal point for Mary and all mankind. She has a decision to make. After all, like all humans, Mary has free will—another important tenet of the Christian faith. God does not force himself upon us. He was not forcing Mary through the angel Gabriel either. The decision was up to her. Mary easily could have said, "Thanks, but no thanks." Just imagine the pressure she was under—the scandal that would erupt when people discovered that the virgin Mary was with child. But Mary trusted her faith. As a very devout Jew, she was certainly aware that God had promised a Messiah. She trusted that God would guide her. In a seemingly unwavering tone, she responded, "Here I am, the Lord's bondslave. Let it be with me as you say." It was as simple as that. There were no consultations with her attorney and no DNA testing as might occur in modern times. Just a trusting, "Yes."

Mary's decision changed the course of human events. This is why Mary is placed in such high esteem—she agreed to carry and give birth to the Son of God! As a Catholic, I am well aware of how some criticize us for our veneration of Mary. For the record, we do not worship Mary. We show her proper respect and venerate her as the Mother of God (John 19:25). Mary exemplifies the Christian qualities we should all aspire to: humility, trust, obedience, faithfulness, and an abiding love of God and neighbor.

Jesus' Life

The Bible tells us all we need to know about Jesus, and countless books have been written on his life. My intention isn't to repeat what's already been written. Instead, in the following sections, I focus on key milestones and messages in the life and times of Jesus and share my own reflections.

Early Childhood

It's worth repeating that Jesus and his family were observant Jews. They practiced their faith as a family. They attended synagogue, observed the holy days, most notably Passover, as well as the rites and rituals associated with their faith. Obviously, religion and religious practices were an important component of the Holy Family's faith.

Though the Bible contains only a couple of references to Jesus' early childhood, we learn that as a twelve-year-old boy, He was deeply immersed in his faith. In what can be classified as the original *Home Alone*, Jesus is inadvertently left behind in Jerusalem following the Passover feast. Families and relatives traveled in large caravans. Mary and Joseph assumed he was somewhere in the caravan, which is easy to understand; it happens often in modern times when large groups of people are traveling to the same destination but in multiple vehicles. "Where's Bill?" "I don't know; we thought he was in your car!" Sound familiar? Imagine traveling for a day and then finding out someone was left behind, especially a young boy from a small village, now wandering around the equivalent of a large city—Jerusalem. I can only imagine the anxiety and panic his parents must have experienced. They travel back to Jerusalem where it took them three days to find him. And where did they find him? He was in the temple, "sitting among the teachers, listening to them and asking them questions. And all who heard Him were astonished at His understanding and His answers" (Luke 2:46–47 KJV).

Message for us: Practicing our faith as a family, including attending services on a regular basis, is essential to being a Christian. This includes all members of the family. A parent (*usually* the dad) often opts out, which sends the wrong message to the kids. They figure, "If dad doesn't go, why should we have to?" Difficult to argue against that. As a result, the church-going parent will usually acquiesce and let the kids stay home with Dad. It's not worth the fight. I realize that a parent may have good reasons to opt out, but I don't think those who do realize the poor example they set. So dads (and some moms), make it a point to attend as a family—it's only about an hour a week. Also, as a twelve-year-old boy, Jesus set a great example for how we should actively participate in our faith—we have to own it. Show some interest, study your faith, and ask questions!

Jesus Prepares for Public Ministry

Following the episode in the temple, we don't hear about Jesus again until he's about thirty years old, which is when he begins his public ministry. Two seminal events occur in close succession to prepare Jesus. The first is his baptism at the Jordan River by John the Baptist—who you may recall was a cousin of Jesus. All four Gospels attest to the baptism in strikingly similar detail. At this point, John is the "big man on campus!" People were drawn by his message of repentance and cleansing via baptism. He's described as wearing clothes made of camel's hair, wearing a leather belt, and eating locusts and wild honey. Somehow, the image of Hagrid from the *Harry Potter* movies comes to mind. He's outspoken with a fiery personality. He doesn't hold back when the Pharisees and Sadducees approach for baptism saying, "You brood of vipers! Who warned you to flee from the coming wrath" (Matthew 3:7 NIV)?

Many thought John might be the Messiah, but he was very clear about his identity and purpose. When Jesus approached to be baptized, John immediately recognized Him as the Messiah. He told Jesus that it was he who should be baptized by Jesus. After all, as the Son of God, Jesus was without sin and in no need of baptism.

> But Jesus answered him, 'Let it be so for now. For in this way, we shall do all that God requires.' So John agreed. As soon as Christ was baptized, he came up out of the water. Then heaven was opened to him, and he saw the Spirit of god coming down like a dove and lighting on him. Then a voice said from heaven, 'This

is my own dear Son, with whom I am pleased'
(Matthew 3:15–17 GNT).

The second seminal event followed very shortly after. Jesus is led into the desert for forty days and forty nights of prayer and fasting. This was followed by the temptation of the devil described earlier in this chapter.

Message for us: How often do we rush the preparation of an important undertaking, whether in our personal or professional life? By His example, Jesus is advising us to take the time to fully prepare ourselves for an endeavor, especially when the stakes are high. This calls to mind the lyrics in a Bob Dylan song: "Know your song well before you start singing it." Jesus studied scripture—he knew it inside and out. He tested his knowledge by asking lots of questions and engaging with others. He prepared himself spiritually, starting with His baptism. He showed tremendous humility in allowing John the Baptist to baptize Him. To John's credit, he also showed great humility by acknowledging Jesus as the Messiah. At one point, he declared, "He (Jesus) must increase while I (John) must decrease" (John 3:30 CSB).

How many of us know when it's time to step back and let another shine? Our ego often gets in the way. John was *the man*. People were flocking to him in droves. He could have easily convinced himself that it was all about him. Maybe he was wrong; maybe he, not Jesus, was the real messiah. But John was too well grounded. He demonstrated humility, which essentially means knowing the truth about oneself. Know what your calling is and when it's time to pass the baton to someone else.

Finally, in the desert, Jesus deprives himself of nourishment and all creature comforts. He engages in total self-sacrifice in order to be completely battle tested for his public ministry. He absorbs himself in prayer to His Father. How willing are we to make sacrifices in life? I'm not sure I could go a full day without food. How about our smartphones? Gossip? Negative thoughts?

Anger? Jealousy? What are you and I willing to sacrifice for the benefit of others?

Jesus Begins His Public Ministry

Jesus first announces his mission on earth at the local synagogue in Nazareth. When He stands up to read scripture, he is handed the book of the prophet Isaiah. He unrolls the scroll and begins to read:

> The Spirit of the Lord is upon me, because he has chosen me to bring good news to the poor. He has sent me to proclaim liberty to the captives and recovery of sight to the blind, to set free the oppressed and announce that the time has come when the Lord will save his people (Luke 4:18–19 GNT).

Jesus then sits down and tells those present, "This passage of scripture has come true today as you heard it being read" (Luke 4:21 GNT). Just as John the Baptist pointed his followers to Jesus, Jesus points His followers to the Father. But this was not Jesus' coming out party. That would officially occur at a wedding in Cana when Jesus turns water into wine. But before that, Jesus has to select and assemble his "A" team—the twelve apostles.

I find two aspects of the selection process intriguing. The first is that Jesus chooses as His team relatively uneducated commoners—fishermen and farmers for the most part. Think about that for a moment. These 12 Jewish men were selected to continue the work of Jesus following His death and resurrection. (Of course, they weren't aware of what they were signing up for at the time!) In the United States, when a new president comes into office, that person assembles a cabinet consisting of 15 members to oversee various executive departments. Those selected are most often a roster of "Who's Who," possessing impressive

academic credentials and well accomplished in the private and/
or public sector. In a public company, members of the Board
are similarly chosen. Yet, Jesus picks what can be called a ragtag
team of ordinary guys, all with very distinct personality traits.
Consider Peter, the Rock—brash, impulsive, wearing his heart on
his sleeve. Matthew was a tax collector whose ilk was despised by
the Jews. Tax collectors during the time of Jesus worked for the
Romans (also despised), currying favor with them. The tax collectors often lined their own pockets by charging the Jews extra
and skimming off the top.

Do you ever wonder why Jesus didn't choose from the edu-
cated rich, powerful, and connected? Or why he didn't choose
from the scholars and teachers of the Jewish Law? Given the way
God chose to bring Jesus into the world, it's pretty easy to see
why. Jesus came into the world, born to parents of modest means
in a barn and placed in a manger. This was no IKEA crib either!
Rather, a manger is a wooden or stone trough used to feed hors-
es or cattle. Jesus, a man of humble background, chose flawed,
down-to-earth men. Of course, it would take him three years to
make them "battle ready."

The second aspect of the selection process I find intriguing is
how the 12 apostles were willing to leave their livelihoods and
families to follow a virtual stranger. The Gospels vary in terms
of exactly who came on-board and when. Jesus, apparently, had
developed some notoriety within the community, and word gets
around. The apostles must have had some idea as to the man and
His message. We can assume that the message resonated with
them. Imagine for a minute if your spouse came home one day
telling you and your children that they were running off to join
a group headed by a religious figure. Today, you'd immediately
think that they were joining a cult.

Message for us: Whether in the workplace or when out socializing, we can easily be tempted to surround ourselves with
influential people. We may brush aside or ignore people we

believe are of a lower social class or find uninteresting. We tend to associate with people who are like us—socially, economically, politically, and so on.

Jesus knew his "team" was not perfect, but He recognized the potential which He helped all but one (Judas) reach. Think about the people you gravitate to when socializing or at work. If you were tasked with assembling a team for a project or sport, who would you select and why? When doing so, it's a good idea to broaden your thinking—you may be pleasantly surprised!

The 12 apostles gave everything up to be with Jesus. It was a complete leap of faith. What are you willing to give up in order to follow Jesus? How forthcoming are you about sharing your faith with others? Do you keep your love for Jesus in the closet? Don't be afraid to profess your belief in God and proclaim what Jesus has done for you—and what He can do for others.

On the Road with Jesus

By now, Jesus has completed His preparation, selected his team, and performed his first miracle—changing water into wine. (The sequence varies among the four Gospels but these events occur in relatively close proximity.) He is now ready to officially commence His ministry. Miracles and wonders are performed everywhere He goes—word spreads quickly, and before long, throngs of people are following him.

During Jesus' time, people believed miracles were a sure sign that those performing them truly possessed supernatural powers. Jesus knew that the miracles and healings were a way to validate Himself as a spokesman, so to speak, for God. He performed healings of people possessed by demons, both literally as in exorcism and figuratively as in mental illness. He cured those plagued with physical ailments—the blind, deaf, deformed, lepers. Unlike others purporting to perform similar healings, Jesus brought the dead back to life, such as in the case with Lazarus. He tamed nature. For instance, Mark's Gospel recounts how Jesus and his disciples were crossing a lake in their boat and a strong wind whipped up. The wildly rocking boat began to take on water. The disciples, fearing for their lives, cried out to a sleeping Jesus to save them. "When Jesus woke up, he rebuked the wind and said to the waves, 'Silence! Be still!' Suddenly the wind stopped, and there was a great calm" (Mark 4:39 NLT).

As a result of the miracles, healings, and feeding thousands with only a few loaves and fishes, Jesus succeeded in attracting enormous crowds. But that was not his main purpose. Yes, people needed to see that Jesus possessed supernatural powers, which could only come from God, and they needed a good reason to come hear him preach—healings and free food! The *primary* purpose, however, was to convey His message of God's love and how to live upright and gain salvation and eternal life through the forgiveness of sins. He needed to spread the word that He was not only the messenger, but one with God who chose Him to be the sacrificial lamb as atonement for the sins of all mankind.

Jesus' Death

Some Christian denominations portray Jesus on the cross in resurrected form. In the Catholic faith, his image is that of the crucified Christ. Neither depiction is wrong, as He was both. The image of the crucified Jesus is a stark reminder of the pain and suffering He experienced for our collective benefit. Crucifixion was a common form of punishment used by the Romans at the time. In Jesus' case, prior to death on the cross, He was savagely scourged with a *flagrum*—a whip consisting of leather thongs with metal or bone attached to the ends. The fierce lashes literally tear the flesh off the body. He was ridiculed, spat upon, slapped, and mocked as "the king of the Jews" and crowned with a headband of sharp thorns.

Finally, he was forced to carry his cross and was nailed to it on Golgotha. The manner in which the Romans nailed the body to the cross made breathing very difficult. This resulted in a slow, painful death by asphyxiation.

As a side note, I find the symbolism of Jesus' death on the cross fascinating. He was truly the fulfillment of prophecy and the keystone of God's plan for us. Consider this: In some Bible translations, Jesus was hanged on a "tree." In Genesis, Adam and Eve ate from the Tree of Knowledge and were banished from the Garden of Eden, which prevented them access to the Tree of Life, the key to eternal life. By allowing Himself to be crucified on a "tree," Jesus redeemed humanity and provided us a path, should we choose to follow it, to eternal life (the Tree of Life).

Just prior to drawing his last breath, Jesus cried out, "Eloi, Eloi, lema sabachtani" (Mark 15:34 NIV)? This translates to, "My God, my God, why have you forsaken me?" This was a cry out from the *human* Jesus. Yes, Jesus was fully human and fully divine. How many times do we cry out to God during times of pain and suffering? Jesus' death on the cross has led many to question why would God allow his only begotten son to suffer such a horrible death? This also leads to a broader question as to why bad things happen to good people.

The Mystery of Suffering

Like Job who suffered greatly, I'm in no position to question why God allows pain and suffering, especially with "good" people. We can trace it back to original sin. As a result of Adam's and Eve's disobedience, all humanity was condemned to pain, suffering, and ultimately death. We also know that Jesus took on our collective sin from the beginning through the end as expiation (atonement for our wrongdoing). It was not forced upon Him—He had free choice, which is what caused His agony in the Garden of Gethsemane. As for us, we don't consciously choose to suffer. Rather, suffering is often a result of choices we make in life or the result of someone else's poor choices.

Suffering can also be foisted upon us as a way to share in Christ's suffering for our own benefit or that of others. St. Paul speaks to this in his second letter to the Corinthians:

> In order to keep me from becoming conceited, I was given a thorn in my flesh, a messenger of Satan, to torment me. Three times I pleaded with the Lord to take it away from me. But He said to me, "My grace is sufficient for you, for my power is made perfect in weakness." Therefore I will boast all the more gladly about my weaknesses, so that Christ's power may rest on me. That is why, for Christ's sake, I delight in weaknesses, in insults, in hardships, in persecutions, in difficulties. For when I am weak, then I am strong (2 Corinthians 12:7–10 NIV).

A few months after my mom turned 89, she began to experience severe health problems. At a low point, when she was going through a particularly difficult period, she asked me, "I don't know what I did wrong to deserve this pain." That led to a discussion about Job who suffered tremendous loss and pain. His friends were sure that God must be punishing him for something he did wrong. As you may be aware, that wasn't the case. Nor was it the case with my mom.

She didn't suffer alone either. My siblings and I were at her side. Seeing her suffer the way she did was difficult for all of us. I prayed often to God that if it was His will to either ease her suffering or allow her to pass peacefully in her sleep. A month or so later, she suffered a massive stroke. Since I had medical power of attorney and mom had a living will, it was clear that she did not want to be kept alive through artificial means. In her case, a permanent feeding tube would have had to be inserted. The doctors also told me that due to the damage to her brain, she wouldn't be able to move or talk—ever.

We decided to honor her wishes and moved her into hospice care. Without food or water, we were told it would be a matter of weeks if not days. The caring, compassionate and experienced staff at the Regional Hospice assured us that mom was comfortable, which was comforting to us. Yet, I still wondered why God would allow her to linger like this and why her loved ones had to be witness to her slow death.

She was unconscious the entire time, but the caretakers told us she could hear and feel our touch. My siblings and I essentially held vigil for the next several days. There were times when each of us was alone with her and other times where several of us were present. We talked to her and prayed with and for her. Some of her closest friends and relatives had an opportunity to visit, as well.

It was during this time that it hit me—mom's suffering was not for her benefit but for ours! As in any family, every child has a different relationship with their parents. Some may have "unfinished business" needing to be addressed. This gave each of us a chance to express ourselves and say our goodbyes.

Four days after entering Hospice care, mom took her last breath. When I called her friend of 86 years to tell her about mom's passing, her first words were, "Your mother was the only true Christian I've ever known. She really lived her faith." As a devout Catholic, there was no question in my mind about her whereabouts—she was with Jesus and reunited with her loved ones.

Indeed, suffering is a mystery. Some experience it much more than others. And some handle it with grace and channel it into something positive. Tennis great Arthur Ashe was the first black player selected to the United States Davis Cup team and the only black man ever to win the singles title at Wimbledon, the US Open, and the Australian Open. In 1992, Ashe publicly disclosed that he had contracted HIV, likely due to a blood transfusion he had received years earlier during a heart bypass. He was 48 years old at the time and would have only a year to live. As reported in *The New York Times* (October 25, 1992), shortly before he passed away, Ashe addressed a packed college auditorium, where in part he said:

> I've had a religious faith, growing up in the South and black and having the church as a focal point of your life. And I was reminded of something Jesus said on the cross: "My God, my God, why hast thou forsaken me?" Remember, Jesus was poor, humble, and of a despised minority. I wasn't poor in that my father was a policeman, but we certainly weren't rich. And Jesus asked the question, in effect, of why must the innocent suffer. And I'm not so innocent—I mean, I'm hardly a perfect human being—but you ask about yourself, "Why me?" And I think, "Why not me?"

Knowing his fate, he went on to found the Arthur Ashe Foundation for the Defeat of AIDS and the Arthur Ashe Institute for Urban Health before his death. On June 20, 1993, Ashe was posthumously awarded the Presidential Medal of Freedom by United States President Bill Clinton.

I can only hope and pray that I can face adversity with the same grace.

Jesus' Resurrection

Up to Jesus' resurrection, we see very little debate about the historical Jesus. Jewish historian, Flavius Josephus (A.D. 37–c. 100), makes many references to Jesus in his book, *The Antiquities of the Jews*. Following is an excerpt from *In the Footsteps of Jesus* by Jean-Pierre Isbouts based on content from Josephus' account of

Jesus' life and resurrection. Isbouts explains that the bracketed text might have been added later by monks who had copied the work:

> "Now, there was about this time Jesus, a wise man [if indeed one might call him a man], for he was a doer of wonderful works, a teacher of such men as receive the truth with pleasure. He drew over to him both many of the Jews and many of the Gentiles. [He was the Christ.] And when Pilate, at the suggestion of the principal men amongst us, had condemned him to the cross, those that loved him at the first did not cease to be attached to him [for he appeared to them alive again the third day as the divine prophets had foretold these and then ten thousand other wonderful concerning him]. And the tribe of Christians, so named from him, are not extinct at this day.

The Koran, which Muslims believe was revealed to the Prophet Muhammad beginning in the year 609, contains about 70 references to Jesus. Though Muslims believe Jesus was a Prophet and a Holy Man, they do not believe he was the Son of God or the Messiah.

With regard to the resurrection, only Christians believe that Jesus rose from the dead on what we celebrate as Easter Sunday. No other faith makes the same claim. This is a crucial tenet of the Christian faith because if Jesus did not rise from the dead, He's viewed as a phony or false prophet. But we Christians believe He truly did rise from the dead. As the saying goes in today's vernacular, "This is a game changer!" (This is also an understatement by far.)

The empty tomb and Jesus' appearance to his disciples and others following his resurrection gave witness to the resurrection.

Though, ultimately, without hard evidence, belief in the resurrection is an act of faith. Jesus kept his promise to his disciples, and God kept his promise to mankind. As a result, no matter what happens in the world, and no matter how big our problems may seem, we can take the long (or eternal) view. We have hope and salvation through Jesus Christ—the Risen Lord!

The Holy Spirit

Following His resurrection, and prior to His ascent into heaven, Jesus promises to send a "helper" or advocate on his behalf: "But the Helper, the Holy Spirit, whom the Father will send in my name, He will teach you all things and bring to your remembrance all that I have said to you" (John 14:26 ESV).

Jesus makes good on his promise as described in dramatic fashion in the Book of Acts:

> When the day of Pentecost arrived, they were all together in one place. And suddenly there came from heaven a sound like a mighty rushing wind, and it filled the entire house where they were sitting. And divided tongues as of fire appeared to them and rested on each one of them. And they were all filled with the Holy Spirit and began to speak in other tongues as the Spirit gave them utterance (Acts 2:1–4 ESV).

Recall that days earlier, Jesus brought Peter, James, and John to the Garden of Gethsemane. There, they witnessed Jesus at His weakest most desperate hour. Shortly after that, He was turned over to the Roman guards, who ultimately led Him to his death. Peter denied knowing him not once or twice, but three times. The rest of the disciples scattered lest they face the same fate.

Following the crucifixion, the disciples were huddled in the upper room fearful and cowering. Then, as Jesus had promised, the disciples were filled with the Holy Spirit. This strikes me as an incredible "about face"! The Holy Spirit emboldened them. All of a sudden they demonstrated an unshakable and unwavering faith. They were fearless and soon after went about their mission to boldly proclaim the "Good News," in spite of the repercussions for doing so. In fact, with the exception of John, they all would eventually meet the same gruesome end as Jesus. Peter is believed to have been crucified upside down—he did not feel worthy of being crucified in the same manner as Jesus.

As a result of the apostles' efforts, the Christian Faith spread and grew exponentially. By some estimates, near the end of the century, there were more than 300,000 Christians, in spite of the persecutions and the best efforts of the forces working to put a stop to the spread of Christianity. Here we are 2,000+ years later, and according to a Pew research study conducted in 2015, there are over 2.3 billion Christians, making it the largest religion in the world.

Indeed, the advice given by the Pharisee named Gamaliel, a teacher of the law, was prophetic. In Acts, we read that the Sanhedrin were gathered to determine how to punish the disciples for teaching about Jesus in public. They were intent on putting a stop to Christianity. At one point, Gamaliel stood up in the Sanhedrin and ordered that the men be put outside for a little while. Then, he addressed the Sanhedrin:

> Men of Israel, consider carefully what you intend to do to these men. Some time ago, Theudas appeared, claiming to be somebody, and about four hundred men rallied to him. He was killed, all his followers were dispersed, and it all came to nothing. After him, Judas the Galilean appeared in the days of the census and led a band of people

in revolt. He too was killed, and all his followers were scattered. Therefore, in the present case I advise you: Leave these men alone! Let them go! For if their purpose or activity is of human origin, it will fail. But if it is from God, you will not be able to stop these men; you will only find yourselves fighting against God (Acts 5:35–39 BSB).

The moral of the story: You'll never win in a fight against God!

Heaven and Eternal Life

Mary Neal, a practicing orthopedic surgeon, had a near-death experience (NDE) about 20 years ago while kayaking in Chile. A drowning accident left her technically dead for about a half hour. During this time, she claims she went to heaven and then returned back to earth. She has written about her experience in the book, *7 Lessons from Heaven*. While I won't be presenting the seven lessons, they are remarkably similar to other accounts I have read about from highly credible people. Many NDEs have similar themes, including intense feelings of peace and unconditional love and reunions with loved ones, who are in perfect health regardless of the severity of their condition on earth prior to death. Most say they view "reruns" of their entire lives in very vivid detail. They describe heaven as a place of exquisite beauty and do not want to leave it when they are hearkened back to earthly life.

In an article appearing in the online magazine, *Mind, Body, Gym*, Mary is quoted as saying:

> I was most astonished by the discovery that God's promises are actually, amazingly, and abundantly true. God is always with us. God always loves us. God's intentions for us are always good. Those

amazing realities can literally change our values and decisions every day. As one who came to faith in adulthood, I had hoped these truths were true, and I nearly always believed that they were. But heaven taught me that we can move beyond hope and belief to something much better and more powerful. We can live with absolute trust. And that can change how you and I live right here on earth.

I realize there are many cynics and skeptics of accounts of NDEs. They claim that the person was not really dead, was hallucinating, or was under the influence of mind-altering drugs. That could be true in some of the accounts. What strikes me, though, is not only the similarity of the accounts but also the sincerity and humility in which they are described. When you have a chance, go to YouTube and search for NDEs. Watching individuals share their compelling stories is quite convincing. Clearly, they have experienced what can only be described as a supernatural phenomenon. In most of the cases I have read, their lives are changed for the better, and they have a renewed sense of purpose.

Those believing in the accounts of NDEs have an opportunity to catch a glimpse of what heaven may be like. For those who don't, the Bible provides "hints" of what heaven is like. Just prior to His crucifixion, Jesus tells His apostles that He will be going away soon. When Peter asks Him where He's going, Jesus says that he (Peter) cannot follow just yet.

Then, in an allusion to His resurrection and ascent into heaven, Jesus shares these words of comfort to His apostles:

> Jesus said, "Do not let your hearts be troubled. You believe in God; believe also in me. My Father's house has many rooms; if that were not

so, would I have told you that I am going there to prepare a place for you? And if I go and prepare a place for you, I will come back and take you to be with me that you also may be where I am. You know the way to the place where I am going."

Thomas said to him, "Lord, we don't know where you are going, so how can we know the way?"

Jesus answered, "I am the way and the truth and the life. No one comes to the Father except through me. If you really know me, you will know my Father as well. From now on, you do know Him and have seen Him" (John 14:1–7 NIV).

I think Jesus wasn't necessarily talking about an actual mansion or compound for that matter. We can infer that heaven is a specific and expansive place that Jesus prepares for us. We also know that those going to heaven will be with God and that He and Jesus are one in the same. Finally, Jesus makes it clear that He is *the* path to the Father.

Jesus also tells us that heaven is a place where our true treasure lies and can never be taken from us: "Do not store up for yourselves treasures on earth, where moths and vermin destroy, and where thieves break in and steal. But store up for yourselves treasures in heaven, where moths and vermin do not destroy, and where thieves do not break in and steal" (Matthew 6:19–20 NIV).

What Happens to Our Bodies?

In terms of what kind of body we will have in heaven, we look to the form Jesus took on following His death and resurrection. When the disciples were huddled in the upper room with the door tightly locked, Jesus appears in their midst. Somehow, He was able to pass through a solid door and yet he was not in the form of a ghost. He showed them His hands and His side, which bore the marks of the wounds He endured during the crucifixion. The next time He appears, He tells Thomas the doubter, "Put your finger here; see my hands. Reach out your hand and put it into my side. Stop doubting and believe" (John 20:27 NIV).

So, not only will we have physical bodies, our health will be perfectly restored, as Paul explains:

> But our citizenship is in heaven. And we eagerly await a Savior from there, the Lord Jesus Christ, who, by the power that enables Him to bring everything under His control, will transform our lowly bodies so that they will be like His glorious body (Philippians 3:20–21 NIV).

Further, we are told that no longer will we experience pain and sorrow:

> And God will wipe away every tear from their eyes; there shall be no more death, nor sorrow, nor crying. There shall be no more pain, for the former things have passed away (Revelation 21:4 NASB).

Good News for "Foodies!"

Soon after showing His apostles that He wasn't a ghost, Jesus made what can be described as the most human of requests:

> And when he had said this, he showed them his hands and his feet. And while they still disbelieved for joy and were marveling, he said to them, 'Have you anything here to eat?' They gave him a piece

of broiled fish, and he took it and ate before them"
(Luke 24:40–43 ESV).

I can only imagine what kind of food awaits in heaven:

> On this mountain the Lord of hosts will make for
> all peoples a feast of rich food, a feast of well-aged
> wine, of rich food full of marrow, of aged wine
> well refined (Isaiah 25:6 ESV).

Yes, you read correctly, *"well-aged wine."*
During the Last Supper, Jesus hands his disciples the cup containing the wine, and after giving thanks to God, says:

> Drink it, all of you. This is my blood which seals
> God's covenant, my blood poured out for many
> for the forgiveness of sins. I tell you I will not
> drink again of this fruit of the vine until that day
> when I drink it new with you in my Father's king-
> dom (Matthew 26:27–29 GNT).

We can read much into the references of heaven in the Bible, but who knows for certain? What we do know from NDEs and Biblical references is that it's a place of pure love and joy. Think of the most wonderful and joyful experiences you've had on earth—celebrations with family and friends, watching a beautiful sunset, walking on the beach. Now, multiply that 1,000 times and remove all the bad stuff that happens in life. Then add the words of Paul, in his letter to the Corinthians:

> That is what the Scriptures mean when they say,
> "No eye has seen, no ear has heard, and no mind
> has imagined what God has prepared for those
> who love him" (1 Corinthians 2:9 NLT).

This may bring you a little closer to what heaven is like.

CHAPTER 8

Getting to Know God

When you have some time, I encourage you to see *Fiddler on the Roof*—the play or the movie. The main character is Tevye, an impoverished milkman in a Jewish community and the father of five daughters. Throughout the play, Tevye carries on a running conversation with God, as though God is his best friend with unlimited time and patience to listen to Tevye's concerns, however insignificant they may seem, soothe his worried mind, and offer His infinite wisdom.

Tevye doesn't exactly engage in formal prayer. His relationship with God is much more intimate and personal. It's the type of relationship we should all strive for as Christians. God should be a constant companion, and He wants to be, if we let Him.

In this chapter, I provide guidance on how to grow closer to God and get to know Him more intimately. As you read, keep in mind that God *wants* to be close to you. He wants to be part of your life. When people feel distant from God, it's they who rejected God, not God who rejected them. Regardless of our past relationship with God, we are always welcome back, just as in the story of "The Prodigal Son."

The Stages of Spiritual Growth

Like physical and intellectual growth, spiritual growth occurs in stages. I like to use a model from human relationships to describe the three distinct phases that bring us closer to God: Attraction, Dating, and Marriage.

Attraction

In the Attraction phase, something piques our curiosity about spirituality. Susan grew up in a Christian household, but her parents weren't particularly devout. Not until a very close friend was diagnosed with a terminal illness did Susan discover faith. She began to read the scriptures and attend Bible study and church services. Throughout the process, she moved slowly into a deeper commitment to God.

As I relate in Chapter 1, I experienced a revitalized attraction to God when I started reading a copy of an abridged Bible that one of my colleagues at the college radio station where we worked had left in a prominent location to entice anyone who happened upon it.

Your Attraction phase may be sparked by a person, an event, a book, a movie, or even divine intervention. God had to practically knock Saul off his horse to get his attention (Acts:9). My hope is that for some readers at least, this book will ignite an attraction to God.

Dating

By the time we have reached the Dating phase, we have sorted out whether or not our initial attraction was simply infatuation. We spend more time reading the Bible and may even participate in formal Bible study. We may start to attend formal church services or increase the frequency of attendance. We try to pray, or we pray more often. We may even read devotionals or religious books or articles.

As the relationship intensifies, we may run into disagreements and conflict. Our faith is challenged. In the face of adversity, some people may choose to abandon the relationship. Those who survive the test of fire emerge with an even stronger faith.

Marriage

Assuming we connect strongly with God during the Dating phase, we eventually make a commitment to follow Jesus Christ and worship God our Father. Anyone who has entered into marriage knows that it is an entirely new level of commitment. It is intended to be lifelong—"Till death do us part." In the spiritual realm, marriage to our faith involves both individual and shared development.

Brad and Teresa attend religious services together and make it a point to pray as a family before meals and at bedtime with the kids. Brad volunteers as a youth minister at his church. Teresa is involved with a weekly Bible study group.

Strengthening their spiritual commitment over time, as in marriage, leads to a maturity not easily subjected to the whims of human nature. Just as in human relationships, the basis for building an enduring, loving relationship with God is through consistent and continual communication. What differs between communicating in a human relationship and communicating with God is that we cannot see God. Some claim to have heard God actually speak directly to them. I don't doubt this for a minute—the Bible is filled with stories in which God speaks directly to certain people, such as Moses and Saul. But for the vast majority of us, our relationship with God *appears* to be restricted to one-way communication. The next section, which comprises most of this chapter, explores methods for getting to know God as you journey through the phases of relationship building.

The Power of Prayer

The most powerful way to know God is through prayer. It is the most intimate form of contact with the Almighty. The benefits are myriad. I came across the following quotation recently that highlights some of the benefits of prayer:

> I tell you that prayer clears the eye, steadies the
> hand, calms the nerve, quickens the judgment,
> strengthens the will, makes the whole [person]
> keen, alert, and sure (Author Unknown).

Scientific research shows that prayer, which includes visualization and various forms of meditation, has a significant impact on our psychological and physical wellbeing. Through prayer, we gain faith, hope, and love, which deliver a host of tangible benefits, as evidenced by the following facts:

- Optimists live up to three times longer and have a greater ability to fight off disease (UCLA, Yale).
- Pessimism lowers the body's immune system and increases the risk of illness (Carnegie-Mellon).
- Prayer, visualization, and meditation are three of the most effective mind-body techniques for lowering heart rate and blood pressure (Harvard).
- Heart patients who said they depended on God for strength were three times more likely to survive (Harvard).
- Patients who were prayed over—without their knowledge—experienced less pain, needed less medication and fewer machines and did not die as frequently as patients who were not prayed for (*Southern Medical Journal*).

While these are all very nice examples of the power of prayer, they represent only the positive side benefits. The primary purpose of prayer is to establish a dynamic two-way dialogue in order to develop an enduring relationship with our Creator. We open up ourselves to His love and seek to understand His will for our lives.

In terms of how we should pray, we once again look to our role model Jesus. Luke's Gospel relates the following:

One day Jesus was praying in a certain place. When he finished, one of his disciples said to him, "Lord, teach us to pray, just as John taught his disciples." Jesus said to them, "When you pray, say: Father, hallowed be your name, your kingdom come. Give us each day our daily bread. Forgive us our sins, for we also forgive everyone who sins against us. And lead us not into temptation" (Luke 11:1-4 NIV).

The Lord's Prayer, or the "Our Father," is perhaps the most widely memorized prayer in the Christian world. Jesus cautioned against using lofty and wordy prayers—The Lord's Prayer is a perfect example of brevity and simplicity. Jesus often implored His disciples to approach the Kingdom of Heaven with the innocence of a child. We also know that prayer was a frequent form of communication with God throughout the Old and New Testaments.

Prayer "ACTS"

The purposes of prayer throughout the Bible vary and can be broken down into four main categories: Adoration, Contrition, Thanksgiving, and Supplication (ACTS). In the following sections, I briefly describe each of these prayer categories.

Adoration

Prayers of adoration show our love and respect for God. We're acknowledging Him as our Creator and Father and praising Him for his holiness, as in this passage:

"The Lord is my strength and my defense; He has become my salvation. He is my God, and I will praise Him, my father's God, and I will exalt Him" (Exodus 15:2 NIV).

This is why Jesus includes, "hallowed be thy name," in the Lord's Prayer. Used as an adjective, "hallowed" means to regard as holy; venerated; sacred. For many Americans, every day is a day of prayer. According to a 2014 Pew Research Center survey, more than half (55%) of Americans say they pray every day. The study doesn't break down the types of prayer, but my guess is that far fewer incorporate adoration into their prayer regimen. If you include yourself in the minority, I urge you to build it into your daily prayer. Your prayer can be informal—whatever comes to mind. As for myself, the words don't often come to me spontaneously. As a result, I tend to use more formal prayer from the Bible. "The Prayer of Manasseh," Verses 1–6 provides a great example:

> Lord Almighty, God of our ancestors, God of Abraham, Isaac, and Jacob, God of their righteous descendants, you created the universe and all the splendor that fills it. The sea obeys your command and never overflows its bounds. The power of your wonderful, glorious name keeps the ocean depths in their place. When you show your power, all creation trembles. Your glorious splendor is overwhelming, and your anger is more than sinners can endure. But the mercy you promise is also greater than we can understand or measure.

The full length prayer is actually a prayer of repentance, seeking forgiveness for sins committed. Many of the prayers in the Bible are actually a combination of two or more "ACTS" form of prayers.

Finally, we should take great pain to avoid consciously or unconsciously taking the name of the Lord in vain. I'm amazed at how many Christians I know who don't think twice about using the Lord's name in anger as in asking God to damn someone or as an exclamation—"OMG!"

Years ago, while working for a consulting firm, I attended a workshop on diversity and inclusion. It was required of all employees. We focused on the importance of respecting others regardless of gender, race, sexual orientation, religion, and other differences. As a Christian, I agree that we should treat all people the way we would like to be treated, "The Golden Rule," or the way they would like to be treated, "The Platinum Rule." I couldn't help to notice though how many people in the firm carelessly used the Lord's name, especially "Jesus Christ," when angry or frustrated. I found this deeply offensive and requested that we should strive to eliminate it from our vocabulary in the office setting. The room fell silent, and the facilitator was at a loss for words. The senior executives somehow could not grasp how that can be offensive and more or less dismissed it. Following the workshop, a coworker and committed Christian tracked me down to thank me for speaking up. He, too, was disappointed at the lack of response. I honestly think that most people don't even realize it when they use the name of the Lord recklessly. I usually call attention to it only when it's coming from a close Christian friend. To some, this may sound preachy, but we violate a commandment when we take the Lord's name in vain.

Contrition

Contrition is a form of prayer used to express our sincere sorrow for sinful behavior and eagerness to atone and be forgiven. This could include asking forgiveness for "good" that we hold back; that is, consciously avoiding helping someone in need, especially when it's within our means. We may avoid performing good acts out of busyness, or carelessness. Jesus drives this point home in what is known as the Parable of Lazarus:

> There was a rich man who was dressed in purple and fine linen and lived in luxury every day. At his gate was laid a beggar named Lazarus, covered with sores and longing to eat what fell from the rich man's table. Even the dogs came and licked his sores.
>
> The time came when the beggar died and the angels carried him to Abraham's side. The rich man also died and was buried. In Hades, where he was in torment, he looked up and saw Abraham far away, with Lazarus by his side. So he called to him, "Father Abraham, have pity on me and send Lazarus to dip the tip of his finger in water and cool my tongue, because I am in agony in this fire."
>
> But Abraham replied, "Son, remember that in your lifetime you received your good things, while Lazarus received bad things, but now he is comforted here and you are in agony. And besides all this, between us and you, a great chasm has been set in place, so that those who want to go from here to you cannot, nor can anyone cross over from there to us" (Luke 16:19–26 NIV).

The rich man did not cause Lazarus' condition on earth. Instead, he ignored the plight of his fellow human being. We should do our best to use *Me Power,* whether it be time, talent, or treasure provided by God to render service to others, especially the less fortunate among us.

The most common type of transgression is when we engage in sinful acts that hurt or violate others. I think of it as the "bad" that we put forth. This type of transgression comes in many different forms, and we are frequently unaware of it. I'm not referring to illegal behavior—that clearly is a sin that jeopardizes our soul. Rather, it's the type of behavior that is more or less normalized, such as engaging in gossip, berating or belittling others, or selfishly pursuing our own self-interests at the expense of others. We find ourselves on either the receiving or giving end of these hurtful behaviors at home, in the workplace, and in our social circles. Consider these words of St. Paul:

> Therefore, each of you must put off falsehood and speak truthfully to your neighbor, for we are all members of one body. "In your anger do not sin": Do not let the sun go down while you are still angry, and do not give the devil a foothold. Anyone who has been stealing must steal no longer, but must work, doing something useful with their own hands, that they may have something to share with those in need. Do not let any unwholesome talk come out of your mouths, but only what is helpful for building others up according to their needs, that it may benefit those who listen. And do not grieve the Holy Spirit of God, with whom you were sealed for the day of redemption. Get rid of all bitterness, rage and anger, brawling and slander, along with every form of malice. Be kind and compassionate to one another, forgiving each other, just as in Christ God forgave you (Ephesians 4:25-32 NIV).

None of us is immune to gossiping, undermining others, seeking revenge, venting our anger, and so on. Recall that Jesus said it's not what we put into our mouths that defiles us, but what comes out of our mouths. I find I must be constantly on guard of this kind of behavior. When I fail to avoid it, I seek forgiveness.

Thanksgiving

One day, while Jesus was traveling on the road to Jerusalem, he was approached by ten lepers requesting to be cleansed. Jesus complied and told them to go show themselves to the priests. While on their way, they were healed. As Luke's Gospel tells it, "One of them, when he saw he was healed, came back, praising God in a loud voice. He threw himself at Jesus' feet and thanked him—and he was a Samaritan" (Luke 17:15-16 NIV). Jesus remarked that only one out of the ten gave thanks to and praise to God—and he was a foreigner no less!

We can all relate to a time when we have offered assistance to someone who then neglected to say, "Thank you." And, yes, there are times when we ourselves have been guilty of the same. We need to be mindful of all the prayers answered by God and be sure to thank Him. We should also be thankful for blessings in general. You've undoubtedly heard of the phrase, "the attitude of gratitude." This suggests that instead of dwelling on our problems in life, we should adopt a mindfulness of everything we are grateful for. We take so much for granted.

As a kid, I remember that whenever my siblings or I complained to my grandmother about something—be it the weather, food, friends who had better toys, or other perceived injustices— she would say, "Just be thankful that you have a roof over your head, food to eat, and friends to play with—there are people in the world far worse off." She knew what it was like to have little in life and experience devastating loss. Her parents had both died when she was 14, and she was raised by her older siblings. She was up every morning at 4:30 to feed the animals and do her chores before school. As an adult, she lost her first child several days after giving birth. The baby, Marilyn Louise, was born healthy. Apparently, the doctor was examining her when all of a sudden he was called to an emergency. In his haste, he somehow broke her neck. My grandparents were devastated.

They later had their second child, Jane Isabelle—my mother. The family was of modest means—they had a small home with just enough income to get by. My grandmother worked at a time when most women did not. What always struck me about my grandmother was that I never heard her complain. She was always grateful for the little she had and admonished us to thank God for not only the big things in life, but also the small. This great attribute rubbed off on my mom who had her fair share of troubles in life. I definitely need to do a better job of following their example!

Recently I heard a song on the radio that had a tremendous impact on me. It's titled "Blessed" by Lucinda Williams. I'll share just a sampling of the lyrics,

> We were blessed by the mystic
>
>> Who turned water into wine
>> We were blessed by the watchmaker
>> Who gave up his time
>> We were blessed by the wounded man
>> Who felt no pain
>> By the wayfaring stranger
>> Who knew our names
>> We were blessed by the homeless man
>> Who showed us the way home
>> Blessed by the hungry man
>> Who filled us with love
>> By the little innocent baby
>> Who taught us the truth
>> We were blessed by the forlorn
>> Forsaken and abused

I highly recommend listening to the song in its entirety. (I purchased it on iTunes.) The song reminded me how we are blessed by people we don't often give thought (or thanks) to. Let's all be more mindful in giving thanks to God for all blessings—large and small—and to one another!

Supplication

"Do not be anxious about anything, but in every situation, by prayer and petition, with thanksgiving, present your requests to God. And the peace of God, which transcends all understanding, will guard your hearts and your minds in Christ Jesus" (Philippians 4:6–7 NIV).

My guess is that prayers of supplication are probably the most common. Supplication involves petitioning God for all kinds of things—a promotion, healthy medical results, safe travels, good grades, healing, acceptance to a college of choice, world peace, winning the lottery—you get the idea. There's absolutely nothing wrong in asking for "stuff," for self and others. Recall Jesus' words:

> Ask and it will be given to you; seek and you will find; knock and the door will be opened to you. For everyone who asks receives; the one who seeks finds; and to the one who knocks, the door will be opened.
>
> Which of you, if your son asks for bread, will give him a stone? Or if he asks for a fish, will give him a snake? If you, then, though you are evil, know how to give good gifts to your children, how much more will your Father in heaven give good gifts to those who ask him (Matthew 7:7–11 NIV)!

This passage does not necessarily mean you'll get anything and everything you ask for. A good friend of mine once complained that when it comes to answering prayers, "God always gets his way!" This actually bothered her and deterred her from petitioning God. Her thinking was that if your request is granted, then it's God's will. If not granted, then it wasn't His will. How and when God chooses to answer our prayers is indeed a mystery, but we shouldn't let that discourage us.

In the classic Christmas movie, *It's a Wonderful Life*, the main character, George Bailey (played by Jimmy Stewart), is sitting at a bar. He had just learned about an enormous amount of money that had gone missing from his building and loan business. As a result, he would be forced to close the family business and possibly face a lengthy jail sentence. In desperation, he offers up a prayer to God. He tells God that although he's not much of a praying man, he would be grateful if God would help him through his troubles. Just as he finishes his prayer, he is punched in the face by a man sitting next to him. It seems that George had insulted the man's wife, the teacher of George's kids. After getting "clocked," George mumbles, "That's what I get for praying." Of course, later in the movie, God indeed answers his prayer. God's method, reasoning, and timing are beyond our comprehension.

Also, keep in mind that God is committed to doing what's best for us, regardless of whether we agree with His assessment of what's best. After all, He is our Father. As children, we often want what's not good for us. We beg our parents for it, and no amount of supplication will sway their better judgement. As young children, we would dart across a busy road to pet a cute puppy unless one of our parents was close by to snag us by the collar. In the same way, our heavenly Father wants only what is best for us. And sometimes we need to suffer. We need to be humbled and taught potentially painful lessons. God is committed to raising good children who are happy and achieve their full potential.

Years ago while in college, I was engaged to a young woman, my "true love." Somewhere along the line, the relationship began to falter. I could see that she was pulling away from me. In desperation, I prayed to God pleading with Him to fix the relationship. I prayed intensely over a long period of time. At one point, I "heard" God say, "Don't worry, everything's going to be alright." I interpreted that as God telling me that we would get back together and eventually marry. The only problem was that things got worse. Eventually, we broke off the engagement. I was devastated, "How could God do this to me after telling me it was going to be alright?" It was incomprehensible to me. After all, Jesus said, "Ask and you shall receive."

Instead of being angry with God, I decided to ask Him for help. I realized that I probably contributed to the breakup. I was possessive and jealous—clearly, not the kinds of attributes needed for a healthy relationship and eventually marriage. Over time, through deep and intense prayer, I changed—for the better. Then I asked God to send me someone I can spend the rest of my life with. Within a short period of time, I met Catherine— now my wife of 27 years! As I reflected back, I realized that had God granted my "wish," it would have been a miserable marriage, likely ending in divorce. Instead, His will was done.

We need to be reminded:

> Who can ever learn the will of God? Human reason is not adequate for the task, and our philosophies tend to mislead us because our mortal bodies weigh our souls down. The body is a temporary structure made of earth, a burden to the active mind. All we can do is make guesses about things on earth; we must struggle to learn about things that are close to us. Who, then, can ever hope to understand heavenly things? No one has ever learned Your will, unless You first gave him Wisdom, and sent Your Holy Spirit down to him. In this way people on earth have been set on the right path, have learned what pleases You, and

have been kept safe by Wisdom (Wisdom 9:13-18 GNT).

Sometimes, we think we know what is best when often times we really don't. This is why whenever I have a prayer request, I always close with, "May Your will be done and not my own."

I can honestly say that throughout my life, God has always answered my prayers—often not in the way I had expected or hoped and not necessarily within my desired timeframe, but He has always delivered.

A Springtime Lesson on Patience

Although I don't like to admit it, patience is not something I'm very good at. I am strong-willed and very determined. I have a tendency to force things to fit my sense of timing and urgency. I am reminded of an incident with my kids many years ago on a warm, breezy spring day. Catherine and I had decided to take our two children, Andrew and Jennifer, to the school athletic field to teach them how to fly a kite. It was a great big field that was perfect for kite flying. Before long, the kite was flying high, and I was dazzling my kids with my kite flying acumen. A proud "dad" moment!

Within minutes though, the winds shifted and forced the kite into the menacing branches of a tall, oak tree that stood on the border of the field. "Oh no, daddy!" Jennifer cried, "Look what happened!" Having some experience in removing kites from the most ferocious kite-eating trees, I reassured her that I would do everything I could to extricate the kite. I tried everything I could—a pull here, a pull there, this angle, that angle, giving it slack, taking up the slack—nothing worked. If anything, my best efforts made it even more tangled.

Sensing that I was about to give up, Jennifer looked up at me with her sweet, trusting eyes and said, "C'mon daddy, you can do it. You can do anything." Gulp. Anybody with a four-year- old knows that in their eyes, you can do anything. You possess super-human powers to do the impossible. I thought to myself, "Okay, Mr. positive thinker, now what do you say? Are you going to tell her that it's impossible and you can't do it?" So I looked her in the eye and did the 'ole *act-as-if*, "Don't worry Jen" I said confidently, "I'll get it down no matter what." So I wrapped the heavy-duty kite string several times around my waist. Pulling with all my might, I tried to free the kite, but it wouldn't budge. Then I leaned back with all my weight until the string broke and I landed on my rear end—the kite remained firmly in place. The string was too heavily entangled in the branches. So I explained to Jennifer that sometimes things don't work out the way you want them. I told her that we would have to leave the kite behind, but looking at the bright side, said, "Think how many people will enjoy the beautiful, multi-colored kite flapping in the wind as they drive by." She agreed, and we decided that we could buy another kite and go out again someday.

The next day on my way to the office, I drove past the tree, and there was the kite, blowing high up in it. It bothered me that, in spite of my best effort, I was unable to get it down. "Defeated by a lousy kite," I thought. Although it wasn't directly on my way to the office, I decided to drive by the tree the next day. I couldn't get it out of my head, and for some reason refused to let go of the hope that I would somehow free that kite. As I drove by, I noticed that something interesting had occurred. The kite, which had been stuck firmly in the top of the tree, had somehow moved down to the mid-point. "Incredible!" I thought to myself. But a closer look revealed that although it had moved, it was still a tangled mess. Still intrigued though, I decided to drive by it the next morning. To my amazement, the kite was gone! Staring with disbelief, I got out of my car and walked to the base of the tree. And to my utter astonishment, there laying on the ground in perfect condition was my kite. It was as if someone placed it there very gently. It seemed impossible because it was such an enormous tree, and the kite was completely entangled. And even if it did free itself, there was no way it could drop straight down through the vast network of limbs, branches, and twigs unharmed. But there it was. I brought it home and showed Jennifer who said matter-of-factly, "See Daddy, I told you could do it!"

As I reflected on the entire experience, I realized that I had learned a powerful lesson about God's timing and patience. It seems that in my life there have been times when, in my determination to get things done, I have made more of a mess out of things. Sometimes when trying to force something or someone, things become more tangled. But by letting go of my will, and surrendering it to God, things seem to work themselves out.

This brought to mind the words of Scottish Baptist Oswald Chambers:

> It is much easier to do something than to trust God; we see the activity and mistake panic for inspiration. When God brings a time of waiting and appears to be unresponsive, don't fill it with busyness; just wait. Wait for God's timing and He will do it without any heartache or disappointment.

By the way, I still have the kite! Finally, and once again in the words of Oswald Chambers:

> For those who have a tendency to only pray to God when wanting something, remember that God wants you to be in a much closer relationship with Himself than simply receiving gifts. He wants you to get to know Him. If you have only come as far as asking God for things, you have never come to the point of understanding the least bit of what surrender really means.

Prayer Insights and Tips

Up to this point, I've shared thoughts on the types (forms) of prayer. Following are insights and tips to enhance your prayer.

There's No One Formula

Discover what works best for you. Ask God for discernment.

Rely on the Holy Spirit

Sometimes the words simply don't come, so turn it over to the Holy Spirit: "In the same way, the Spirit helps us in our weakness. We do not know what we ought to pray for, but the Spirit himself intercedes for us through wordless groans" (Romans 8:26 NIV).

Make Prayer a Habit but *Not* a Routine

Formulaic or rote prayers can be helpful but sometimes lose their meaning. Change it up.

Match the Intensity of Prayer with the Gravity of the Situation

Mark's Gospel includes an account of the disciples unable to heal a young boy tortured by an unclean spirit. When Jesus heals the boy, "His disciples asked him privately, 'Why couldn't we drive it out?' Jesus told them, 'This kind can come out only by prayer and fasting' (Mark 9:28–29 BSB)." Based on other examples of Jesus' prayer life, I take from this statement that we need to go "deep" in prayer. I've personally found that fasting for a brief period of time prior to prayer somehow helps me to connect with God on a deeper level. Perhaps by depriving ourselves of carnal delights, we're better able to focus on feeding the soul.

Pray and Worship in "Spirit and Truth"

Jesus reminds us in a sense not to be casual in our worship of God, "The hour is coming, and is now here, when the true worshipers will worship the Father in spirit and truth, for the Father is seeking such people to worship him. God is spirit, and those who worship him must worship in spirit and truth" (John 4:23–24 NLT).

Create or Enter a Setting Conducive to Individual Prayer

Jesus offers the following guideline, "But when you pray, go into your room, close the door and pray to your Father, who is unseen. Then your Father, who sees what is done in secret, will reward you" (Matthew 6:6 NIV). I believe what Jesus means is that we should find a private place to pray where no one else is watching. For me, the "secret" place could be in the church when it's empty or a room in my house when no one is at home. My favorite secret place is in a nature preserve a short drive from where I live. I go deep into the woods and find a good spot off the beaten path. Jesus often went to an isolated spot in nature—on a mountain, in the desert, or near the sea—to commune with his Father.

Engage Regularly in Communal Prayer (Community Worship)

Though I'm much more comfortable with private, individual prayer, we should also engage in communal prayer. Formally, we do this each week during church services. But informally, we sometimes need to come together and pray as members of the Body of Christ. In such cases, Jesus is truly present, "Again, truly I tell you that if two of you on earth agree about anything they ask for, it will be done for them by my Father in heaven. For where two or three gather in my name, there am I with them" (Matthew 18:19–20 NIV).

Engage in Both Verbal and Non-Verbal Prayer

In the "attraction" and "dating" phase as described near the beginning of this chapter, verbal prayer is often the method employed. It deals more with the intellect and operates on a conscious level.

As a person matures in their relationship with God (the "marriage" phase), non-verbal prayer is a powerful way to become one with God. In the early stages of human relationships, such as in the dating phase, we tend to talk a lot. We're learning about each other and getting to know one another better. As the relationship matures, many people find they can be together and be happy in silence.

Catherine and I walk five miles almost every Sunday in an area described as "horse country." The scenery is beautiful any time of the year. On some of our walks, we barely utter a word. Couples married for many years tend to finish the sentences of their spouses because they have become so familiar with each other's thinking. Non-verbal prayer is a higher form of prayer and takes time to develop. It's drawn from the heart (versus intellect) and usually operates at the subconscious level.

I've also learned techniques from other religions. For instance, I've found Eastern methods and techniques helpful, particularly Hinduism with a spiritual focus on meditation. However, as a Christian, my meditation centers around the life, death, and resurrection of Jesus Christ. To avoid any confusion, I'm not suggesting that we should ditch verbal prayer altogether—it definitely plays an important role in our spiritual development. There's no magic ratio, but I found that over time, my non-verbal prayer has increased significantly.

Appreciate the Sounds of Silence

Non-verbal prayer is not silent; it has sounds, the sounds of silence. Sometimes it's sufficient to quiet the mind and stand, kneel, or sit in the presence of God. No agenda. Ask the Holy Spirit for help. Listen. God speaks to us in the silence. But listen closely for He speaks in a gentle whisper, as he did with Elijah:

> The Lord said, "Go out and stand on the mountain
> in the presence of the Lord, for the Lord is about

to pass by." Then a great and powerful wind tore the mountains apart and shattered the rocks before the Lord, but the Lord was not in the wind. After the wind there was an earthquake, but the Lord was not in the earthquake. After the earthquake came a fire, but the Lord was not in the fire. And after the fire came a gentle whisper (1 Kings 19:11–12 NIV).

These insights and tips are based on a combination of Biblical principles and my own experience during my faith journey. I've drawn from many different sources over the years and suggest you do the same. The one thing I can say for certain is that the effectiveness and quality of your prayer life are equal to the proportion of time and energy you invest in developing it.

CHAPTER 9

What Jesus Teaches Us: Seven Key Themes

I n addition to being God's only Son, Jesus is the greatest teacher who ever lived. He employed numerous teaching methods to engage His audience, drive home important life lessons, and transform people's thinking and behavior, including the following:

- By example: As captured in the stories told about Him in the New Testament, especially in the four Gospels, Jesus lived an exemplary life. He showed us how to be Christians.
- Symbolic acts: Jesus often used symbolic acts, such as washing the feet of His disciples, dining with tax collectors, and expelling merchants from the temple.
- Parables: Jesus told simple, often fictional stories that revealed much deeper insights.
- Metaphors and hyperbole: Jesus often used exaggerated comparisons to make a point, such as stating that "it is easier for a camel to pass through the eye of a needle than for a rich person to enter the kingdom of God" (Matthew 19:24 NLT) and admonishing us to remove the plank from our own eye before seeking to remove the speck from another's eye.
- Miracles: He often used the miracles He performed as teachable moments. For example, when Peter began to

doubt that he could walk on water and, as a result, began to sink, Jesus caught him and said, "You of little faith, why did you doubt" (Matthew 14:31 NASB)?

- Questions/dialogue: Like Socrates, Jesus often led people to discover truth on their own by asking them questions, often rhetorical questions, and frequently engaging them in dialogue. For example, Jesus asked, "Who of you by worrying can add a single hour to his life" (Matthew 6:27 BSB)?

In a way, Jesus also employed the technique of rote learning—teaching through repetition. Much of His teachings repeated important themes—lessons that He obviously thought we needed to learn. In this chapter, I highlight seven key themes repeated throughout the Gospels, along with a brief reflection on each.

Love

When asked which is the greatest commandment, Jesus replies:

> Love the Lord your God with all your heart and with all your soul and with all your mind. This is the first and greatest commandment. And the second is like it: Love your neighbor as yourself. All the Law and the Prophets hang on these two commandments (Matthew 22:37-40 NIV).

At this point, Jesus does not provide detail on the meaning of "love." Regarding the love of God, it's safe to say that we should keep Him foremost in our thoughts every day. It also means we should strive to follow His commandments as passed down to Moses.

Remember, Jesus said he did not come to abolish the law—only to fulfill it (Matthew 5:17). The first three commandments relate to the love of God. The next seven relate to love of neighbor/others. With love of neighbor, Jesus reminds us that this includes a love of enemies. Frankly, I don't know about you, but for me, this is the most difficult "directive" to follow. When somebody hurts me or a loved one, my human nature tells me to hurt back—or at the very least hold a long grudge against that person. But Jesus tells us to "turn the other cheek." I understand the principle behind this—Jesus reminds us that it's easy to love people we are close to, but that loving a stranger or someone who brings harm (or simply annoys us) is what we are called to do.

Gandhi adopted this thinking, translating it to passive resistance, as did Martin Luther King Jr. We see Jesus living this truth when he forgives those who have tortured and crucified him. In His dying breath he says, "Father, forgive them, for they do not know what they are doing" (Luke 23:34 NIV). This brings "forgiveness" into the love of neighbor equation. When teaching his disciples how to pray (The Lord's Prayer), he includes "forgive us our trespasses as we forgive those who trespass against us," which is another hard lesson for many. Some people hold grudges against others for life. Fortunately for me, forgiving others is easier. This is partly due to the fact that I have a short memory—often I forget why I'm upset with someone in the first place! I have a harder time forgiving myself for offenses I've committed against others.

I realize that many people have been deeply hurt—especially those experiencing physical or mental violence and abuse. According to a news article appearing in the *New York Post*, Dean Otto of Charlotte, North Carolina was out for an early morning bike ride when an F-150 truck smashed into him. When Otto regained consciousness, he couldn't feel or move his legs. The doctor in the ER gave him only a 2% chance of ever walking again. His vertebrae were smashed against his spinal cord, his back was dislocated, and he suffered a broken pelvis, ribs, and tailbone. But Otto said he did not harbor any resentment toward the driver

206 . SCOTT VENTRELLA

who struck him. Instead, he said a prayer and instantly forgave him. The doctors and surgeons knew if he were to have a chance to walk again, they would have to operate immediately. Though the recovery was long and painful, it was a success. The following year, on the anniversary of the accident, Otto ran a half-marathon (13.1 miles)—along with his surgeon *and the young man who struck him!* Otto claims he owes his miraculous recovery to the power of forgiveness.

In a much more tragic incident in 2015, white supremacist Dylan Roof opened fire in an African American church in Charleston, South Carolina during Bible study, killing nine members of the close-knit congregation. What I found amazing is that during Roof's bond hearings, when given a chance to address him, most family members and relatives forgave him. In the words of Nadine Collier, daughter of victim Ethel Lance:

> I forgive you. You took something very precious away from me. I will never get to talk to her ever again. I will never be able to hold her again, but I forgive you, and have mercy on your soul. . . . You hurt me. You hurt a lot of people. If God forgives you, I forgive you.

Honestly, I don't know how they were able to forgive in such tragic circumstances, but that's what we're called to do. No matter the offense, Jesus is very clear: "But if you do not forgive others their sins, your Father will not forgive your sins" (Matthew 6:15 NIV). In very hurtful situations, ask the Holy Spirit to help you. Talking it over with clergy or a spiritual advisor can also be helpful.

One final aspect of loving others is the idea of serving. The most powerful example of this is what is known as the "washing of the feet," which occurred during the Passover meal the evening before Jesus' crucifixion. Jesus washes the feet of each of His disciples, one after the other. When He had finished, He returned to His place and said to them:

> Do you understand what I have done for you? You call me "Teacher" and "Lord," and rightly so, for that is what I am. Now that I, your Lord and Teacher, have washed your feet, you also should wash one another's feet. I have set you an example that you should do as I have done for you. Very truly I tell you, no servant is greater than his master, nor is a messenger greater than the one who sent him. Now that you know these things, you will be blessed if you do them (John 13:12-17 NIV).

Talk about a teachable moment! Moments earlier, the disciples were arguing amongst themselves who was the greatest. In this act of great humility, Jesus set them all straight.

Faith

I think most Christians find it fairly easy to have and profess our faith—especially when life is running smoothly. The real test of faith is when the going gets rough. Take for instance the account of Jesus walking on the water to join several of his disciples who were out on a boat fishing:

> Shortly before dawn Jesus went out to them, walking on the lake. When the disciples saw him walking on the lake, they were terrified. "It's a ghost," they said, and cried out in fear. But Jesus immediately said to them: "Take courage! It is I. Don't be afraid." "Lord, if it's you," Peter replied, "tell me to come to you on the water." "Come," He said. Then Peter got down out of the boat, walked

on the water and came toward Jesus. But when
he saw the wind, he was afraid and, beginning to
sink, cried out, "Lord, save me!" Immediately, Jesus reached out his hand and caught him. "You of
little faith," he said, "why did you doubt" (Matthew 14:25–31 NIV)?

I keep this image in mind every time my faith begins to falter.
Peter had faith enough in Jesus to step out on the choppy waters.
As long as his gaze was fixed on Jesus, he was fine, but as soon
as he started to pay attention to the raging winds and water, he
panicked and began to sink. What a great lesson Jesus teaches us
here. When life's challenges begin to close in on us, we need re-
fix our gaze on Jesus—and *trust* him.

Faith and trust go hand-in-hand. This is best illustrated in the
story of the mountain climber. Just short of reaching the sum-
mit, he loses his footing. Just before plummeting to sure death,
he grabs hold of a branch. Knowing he cannot hold on for long,
out of desperation he shouts up at the top of the mountain, "Is
there anybody up there? I need help—please somebody help
me!" Miraculously, a voice shouts back, "Yes, I'm up here and I
can help but you have to do what I say." The climber shouts back,
"Thank you! Who is this?" The reply comes back, "It's me, God."
The climber says, "Oh, thank you, God! What do you need me to
do?" God says, "Let go of the branch. . . ." The climber thinks for
a minute, then shouts back up, "Is there anybody else up there
who can help?!"

I can certainly relate to the climber. It's one thing to have faith
and belief in God. It's a whole other thing to have 100% trust
in him. The Roman Officer in Matthew's Gospel is a perfect example of complete trust. I'll paraphrase here: His servant is very
sick. He approaches Jesus some distance from his home, asking
Him whether He could heal his servant. Jesus says He can. But
the officer explains that because of his position and authority, he

does not feel worthy of having Jesus enter his home. Instead, he asks Jesus to simply give the order and his servant will be healed. When Jesus heard this, He was amazed and said to those following him, "Truly I tell you, I have not found anyone in Israel with such great faith" (Matthew 8:10 NIV). When the officer returned home, he found his servant had been healed at the same time he asked Jesus to give the order.

According to Jesus, all we need is faith the size of a mustard seed. It is one of the smallest seeds you'll ever see, yet when it germinates and takes root, it grows into a bush up to 30 feet tall! It's common for people to want some kind of proof before they believe. Thomas, for instance, did not believe that Jesus had risen from the dead. He had his doubts, in spite of eyewitness accounts from his closest, most trusted friends. He essentially tells them, "I'll believe it when I see it!" Shortly afterwards he encounters the risen Lord who shows the "doubter" His open wounds in hands, feet, and side. It is only then that Thomas believes. What does Jesus say to him?

> Because you have seen me, you have believed; blessed are those who have not seen and yet have believed (John 20:29 NIV).

Be careful not to put God to the test by asking for proof. As Jesus told the devil in the desert, "It is said, 'Do not put the Lord your God to the test'" (Luke 4:12 NIV).

Simplicity

Gary Larson is famous for his one frame comics known as *The Far Side*. One of my favorites shows a woman whose husband apparently died recently. The frame shows all kinds of material possessions going out the window and up into the clouds. The comic reads, "Yep, there he goes; he's taking it all with him!" Only in a comic strip!

We live in a very consumer-oriented, materialistic society. Jesus warns us repeatedly not to become too attached to our possessions. The Gospel of Matthew relates the story of the young rich man who asked Jesus what he must do to achieve eternal life. Jesus tells him to obey the Ten Commandments to which the young man agrees. Then Jesus tells him:

> "If you want to be perfect, go, sell your possessions and give to the poor, and you will have treasure in heaven. Then come, follow me." When the young man heard this, he went away sad, because he had great wealth. Then Jesus said to his disciples, "Truly I tell you, it is hard for someone who is rich to enter the kingdom of heaven. Again I tell you, it is easier for a camel to go through the eye of a needle than for someone who is rich to enter the kingdom of God (Matthew 19:21–24 NIV).

The message here is that whether rich or poor (and everything in-between), we can become so attached to things that we lose sight of what's most important in life. This is most starkly noted during the Christmas season where crazed shoppers get caught up in a buying frenzy—losing sight of the whole reason for the season. Many years ago my younger brother's class had a Christmas grab bag. My brother picked a gift that came from a classmate whose family had escaped from the turmoil in Lebanon. The family was of very modest means and unable to afford to buy gifts. The gift was a small boat that was hand carved out of soap. With its intricate detail, you could clearly see that it was carefully carved out of a heart filled with love. It elicited some chuckles from my brother's classmates who also ribbed him, "Ha, all you got was a piece of soap!" For Christmas, just a few days later, my brother received all kinds of cool toys and electronic gadgets. As the weeks passed, most of his Christmas presents were lost, broken, or forgotten. One day I remember coming home and wouldn't you know it—my brother was playing with the ship. It had outlasted all the other gifts! He held onto it for quite a long time after that. That was a long time ago, but the memory really stuck with me.

Jesus does not begrudge us from having nice things. Rather, He cautions us not to become possessed by our possessions. Jesus told his followers not to become preoccupied with wealth and material things—including food and clothes. He admonished them instead to, "Seek ye first the Kingdom of God, and his righteousness; and all these things shall be added unto you" (Matthew 6:33 KJV).

Repentance

In the parable of the Pharisee and tax collector, both men go to the temple to pray. The Pharisee looks down on the tax collector and instead of humbly confessing his sins, the Pharisee extols his own virtue proudly separating himself from evildoers such as the tax collector. Meanwhile, "The tax collector stood at a distance. He would not even look up to heaven, but beat his breast and said, 'God, have mercy on me, a sinner'" (Luke 18:13 NIV).

Some time ago, when discussing faith with a friend, the topic of sin and the need to confess one's sin came up. He proclaimed that he was not in need of repentance since he doesn't sin. I didn't press the matter with my friend. There are many people who truly believe they are without sin. There are two points I'd like to make here. First, we all have the stain of original sin, and second, none of us is immune to sin. Anytime we break a commandment, we sin. Jesus reminds us that impure thoughts are a form of sin—in spite of not acting on them. In a controversial interview appearing in *Playboy* magazine (of all places), former

President Jimmy Carter stated that he had committed adultery many times. In part, he told his interviewer:

> Christ said, "I tell you that anyone who looks on a woman with lust has in his heart already committed adultery." I've looked on a lot of women with lust. I've committed adultery in my heart many times. This is something that God recognizes I will do—and I have done it—and God forgives me for it.

Of course, God forgives him because he has acknowledged and confessed his sin. Simply put, sin separates us from God:

> Your iniquities have made a separation between you and your God, and your sins have hidden His face from you so that He does not hear (Isaiah 59:2 ESV).

As a kid, we used to go to confession on a monthly basis—this is what Catholics did at the time. Today, Confession (or Reconciliation) has grown out of favor—fewer people seem to feel the need to confess one's sins. Non-Catholics claim that you don't need to confess to a priest to have your sins forgiven. I actually agree (even though this is at odds with the Church). Only Jesus can forgive our sins. That said, I still go to confession a few times each year. In my church, you have the option of confessing in anonymity (the priest cannot see you) or face-to face. I prefer face-to-face. For me, there's something special about expressing my sins to another person, in this case, a priest, in a less formal setting. Not only do I hear myself, but the priest invariably offers insightful guidance. It's more like a conversation that I find very helpful. Confession commences with penance as a way to atone for sin and as an Act of Contrition:

Oh my God, I am heartily sorry for having offended Thee. I detest all my sins because of Thy just punishments, but most of all because I offend Thee my God who are all good and deserving of all my love. I firmly resolve, with the help of Thy grace to sin no more and avoid the near occasion of sin.

In the Catholic faith, we also collectively confess our sins at the beginning of every service. It's a general confession beginning with the following:

I confess to Almighty God and to you my brothers and sister that I have greatly sinned. In my thoughts and in my words, in what I have done and what I have failed to do. . . .

In addition to occasional confession with a priest and the general, collective confession during the Mass, I find regular private confession extremely beneficial. Without regular contemplation, I find that sins can buildup over time. During private confession, I begin with a brief examination of conscience. This involves thinking about not only acts of commission, but acts of omission as well. I find it helpful to be specific with God by stating examples. I also keep a journal where I "write out" sins, both general and specific, and include an Act of Contrition—usually by reading Psalm 51, which is powerful. I encourage you to look it up.

In the Jewish faith, Yom Kippur, "The Day of Atonement," is the holiest day on the Jewish calendar. It's a time set aside to repent for sins and to reflect on the year past and the year to come. Observant Jews generally attend synagogue, read from the Torah, and fast for 24 hours.

"If we confess our sins, He is faithful and righteous to forgive us our sins and cleanse us from all unrighteousness" (1 John 1:9 NIV).

Regardless of how egregious, all sins are forgivable, except blasphemy against the Holy Spirit (see Mark 3), as long as you are genuinely sorry and repent from your heart. Instead of hiding from our sins or ignoring them altogether, we should confess them. I've shared methods that have helped me—find out what works best for you.

Judging Others

I touched on the topic of judgment in Chapter 4, in which I briefly discussed the story of the woman caught in the act of adultery, whom the Pharisees thought should be stoned, but would like to make a few additional points. Jesus cautions us to be careful not to judge others:

> Do not judge, or you too will be judged. For in the same way you judge others, you will be judged, and with the measure you use, it will be measured to you. Why do you look at the speck of sawdust in your brother's eye and pay no attention to the plank in your own eye? How can you say to your brother, "Let me take the speck out of your eye," when all the time there is a plank in your own eye? You hypocrite, first take the plank out of your own eye, and then you will see clearly to remove the speck from your brother's eye (Matthew 7:1-5 NIV).

Some interpret this to mean we should not recognize or call out sinful behavior, "Who am I to judge?" In fact, Jesus admonishes us to be very cautious before judging someone else. We need to make sure our own hands are clean lest we be guilty of hypocrisy and be sure that our vision is clear for "if the blind lead the blind, both will fall into the pit" (Matthew 15:14 ESV).

We are certainly obliged at times to acknowledge and correct the wrongdoings of others. Jesus certainly called out those guilty of wrongdoing; consider his righteous anger against the merchants in His Father's temple, and the way He much more gently corrected his disciples and other good people who made mistakes.

When judging others, we are advised to be "slow to anger" and, in most cases, diplomatic; for example, by bringing up issues in private and not berating the other person. We also need to avoid talking about other people's flaws and mistakes behind their backs. The Golden Rule applies especially to judgment—how would you like to be treated by someone who felt the need to point out one of your faults or weaknesses?

"Wolves and Weeds"

Jesus calls special attention to people among us who are under the influence of evil and whom we would be wise to avoid, lest they lead us astray or harm us. These are the people commonly compared to wolves and weeds. He describes each, so that we may be more discerning in our judgment of people:

- Jesus warns, "Beware of false prophets, who come to you in sheep's clothing but inwardly are ravenous wolves. You will recognize them by their fruits" (Matthew 7:15–16 NIV). The "fruits" are the actions and subsequent consequences of such behavior.
- In the parable of the weeds (Matthew 13:24–29), Jesus speaks of "good" seed producing wheat and "bad" seed producing weeds. The good seed is that which God planted. The evil seed is planted by His enemy, the devil. In the parable, the farmer who planted the good seed allows

the weeds and wheat to grow together. At harvest time, he orders that the weeds be pulled up and burned and the wheat harvested and stored in his barn—a clear reference to a final judgment day.

With the help of the Holy Spirit, we can discern the wolves and the weeds in our midst. This act of discernment is a form of judgment. We must be able to judge others in this way to distance ourselves from the evil in the world.

Meekness, Not Weakness

In the Sermon on the Mount, Jesus makes a number of bold pronouncements, aka "The Beatitudes." In his third beatitude he says, "Blessed are the meek for they shall inherit the earth" (Matthew 5:5 NIV).

Meekness for most people carries a negative connotation. A meek person is often thought of as timid, cowering, spineless individual—otherwise referred to as a wimp.

In fact, the word meek comes from the Greek, "Praus." In the secular use of the word, it means to tame wild animals. Being meek means having control over one's strength. A great poem by Mary Karr provides a Christian interpretation:

Who the Meek Are Not

> Not the bristle-bearded Igors bent
> under burlap sacks, not peasants knee-deep
> in the rice-paddy muck,
> nor the serfs whose quarter-moon sickles
> make the wheat fall in waves
> they don't get to eat. My friend the Franciscan
> nun says we misread

that word *meek* in the Bible verse that blesses
them.

> To understand the meek
> (she says) picture a great stallion at full gallop
> in a meadow, who—
> at his master's voice—seizes up to a stunned
> but instant halt.
> So with the strain of holding that great power
> in check, the muscles
> along the arched neck keep eddying,
> and only the velvet ears
> prick forward, awaiting the next order.

Focused Energy

The stallion in the poem is an apropos analogy. Equestrians know that the horse they ride has tremendous power but does not demonstrate it until given the command. The rider "directs" the horse via bridle which includes the headstall, bit, and reins. We can think of meekness as power that is restrained until it becomes necessary to channel it for a good and noble cause. As Christians, God is the rider and we, the meek, are the horse. Once given the command, we should not hesitate to channel our inner power and "fight the good fight."

Redemption

Though at odds with all the major religions, we Christians believe that we can be redeemed only through Jesus Christ. He is the only one who can restore the broken relationship with God, "I am the way and the truth and the life. No one comes to the Father except through me" (John 14:6 NIV).

Billy Graham put it this way:

> This is why I urge you to turn to Jesus Christ, for
> he was God in human flesh, sent from Heaven to
> open the way to God. Only one thing separates
> us from God, and that is our sin—and we cannot
> erase our sins by our own efforts. But by his death
> on the cross, Christ became the final sacrifice for
> our sins.

Be careful however not to judge those who have not accepted Jesus Christ as their Savior. Millions of people have not even heard of Jesus and/or have not had the opportunity to learn about Him and what He has done for humanity. All of the major religions contain messages and truth(s) that can be attributed to the one true God. As Christians, we are called to witness to our faith and at the same time be respectful of others and their respective belief systems.

I just recently read a fascinating book, *Seeking Allah, Finding Jesus*. It's a true story about a devout Muslim, Nabeel Qureshi, who with the help of a devout Christian friend, eventually converts to Christianity. There's much to the story in this book, which I highly recommend. If nothing else, it provides a great template for how to have respectful conversations with people of different faiths (or belief systems within the same faith). Only God knows what's in the hearts and minds of his people. Ultimately, He will render the final judgment—it's not our job to convict or condemn another human being for their conception of God and their unique relationship with Him.

CHAPTER 10

Faith Works!

No doubt, you've heard the expression, "God works in mysterious ways." What is not so mysterious is that for God to have a positive impact on our lives, we must allow Him to do so. After all, God has granted us free will. He will call us to Him, but we must choose to recognize and acknowledge His calling. He will knock, but we must open the door.

In this chapter, I present several conversion stories—stories about real people who have chosen to be receptive to God's calling. As you read the stories, I encourage you to look for two common threads. The first is that the main character in each story has faith—perhaps only a mustard seed of faith, but enough faith to remain open to God's calling. The second is that each person ultimately harnesses the power of Me, We, and Thee—The 3rd Power.

I want you to notice in these stories that each person's faith journey is unique and that they certainly do not harness the power of Me, We, and Thee in the same sequence. Often, Thee power comes first; God intervenes in our lives, encouraging us to look inward (Me Power) to develop deeper insight into who we are and question who we are and what we should be doing with our lives. Sometimes, other people (We Power) lead us closer to God (Thee Power). And, frequently, as we optimize our Me Power and Thee Power, we begin to harness We Power by reaching out to others to lead them closer to God and to multiply the power of good in the world. The three powers are not necessarily sequential, and they are always manifested in unique ways, but the three always combine for maximum positive impact.

My hope is that these stories will further inspire the faithful to continue on their journeys and make the unfaithful or uncertain more receptive to God's calling (and God never stops calling). I further hope that as God calls, you find in this book the guidance you need to respond and harness the full force of The 3rd Power in your life!

Unbroken

Louis Zamperini, whose story is told in the bestselling book *Unbroken*, was an American soldier in WWII. His B-24 bomber experienced a mechanical malfunction, plunking him and his fellow airmen into the Pacific Ocean. With the plane submerged, Louis desperately tried to escape, but he was tangled up in wires and cables. Though he was not particularly religious, he prayed to God, saying that if he survived, he would dedicate his life to Him.

Louis survived not only the crash, but also weeks adrift in the ocean and two years in a Japanese POW camp. He was savagely beaten and tortured by a notorious sergeant overseeing the camp called "The Bird." His captors were aware that he had been a distance runner in the Olympics, so they took special pleasure in beating his legs and feet.

Miraculously, Louis survived the ordeal. After his return to the U.S. following the war, he fell into depression and alcoholism. Understandably, he was angry and bitter. His heart was so filled with hatred toward his captors that he wanted to go back and kill them. Eventually, his wife persuaded him to attend a Billy Graham revival. There, he remembered his pledge to God and made a new commitment to Jesus Christ.

During one of his frequent speaking appearances, Zamperini was quoted as saying, "I have accepted Christ, and from now on I am going to be an honest-to-God Christian."

Having dedicated the rest of his life to God, he decided to help boys and young men "come to Christ" and eventually started a camp for troubled youth—the Victory Boys Camp. As with most people, after re-committing his life to Jesus, he became a new man; he stopped drinking, the nightmares that had tormented him for so many years ceased, and, amazingly, his desire for vengeance left him completely.

Instead of seeking vengeance, Louis found forgiveness and later met with many of his tormentors. In 1952, he returned to Tokyo and visited the Sugamo prison. Now, it held Japanese war criminals, although some of the guards were the same men employed at the prison when Louis had been held captive there. He asked to meet with his former guards individually. Many of them agreed to his request. He greeted them and gave witness to Jesus—as a result, most of them converted to Christianity.

One of his former guards was perplexed and asked Louis how he could forgive his former captors who had treated him so harshly. Louis told him, "Well, Mr. Sasaki, the greatest story of forgiveness the world's ever known was the Cross. When Christ was crucified He said, 'Forgive them Father, they know not what they do.' And I say, 'It is only through the Cross that I can come back here and say this, but I do forgive you. '"

As I've mentioned before, the most difficult teaching of Jesus for me is to "love your enemies and pray for those who persecute you" (Matthew 5:44 NIV). I've read the book, *Unbroken*, and saw the move based on it. I have understated the brutality Louis was subjected to. As a result of his injuries, Louis, who was a star runner and athlete, competing in the 1939 Olympics in Berlin, was never able to compete again. As an avid runner, I can only hope and pray that I could find forgiveness in my heart if someone were to take away my ability to run.

Ultimately, Louis inspired tens of thousands of people to turn back toward their faith—right up until he was called "home" at the ripe age of 97.

Many people walking amongst us have compelling faith stories. They may not have written books or had movies made about their lives, but they serve as living, breathing "witnesses" to the power of faith. Once we completely surrender ourselves to Jesus and accept Him into our lives, we are *never* the *same*.

Saul and the Road to Damascus

The story of Saul is a great example of how Thee Power can intervene in a person's life, transform the person from within (Me Power), and lead others to a closer relationship with God (We Power). Saul enters the scene shortly after Jesus' death and resurrection. The number of disciples was growing rapidly. In the book of Acts, we learn, "Stephen a man richly blessed by God and full of power, performed great miracles and wonders among the people" (Acts 6:8 GNT).

Following his arrest on bogus charges, he lambasted the Council, consisting of Jewish leaders, elders, and teachers of the Law. This infuriated the Council, who, in their rage, ejected Stephen from the city and stoned him to death. Present at the stoning was a young man from Tarsus named Saul. We are told that following the stoning:

> Saul approved of his murder. It was on that very day the church in Jerusalem began to suffer cruel persecution. All the believers, except the apostles, were scattered throughout the provinces of Judea and Samaria. Some devout men buried Stephen, mourning for him with loud cries. But Saul tried to destroy the church; going from house to house, he dragged out the believers, both men

and women, and threw them into jail (Acts 8:1–3 GNT).

As the apostles continued their work with zeal, Saul stepped up his efforts, making violent threats of murder against the followers of Jesus. By now, you know what followed—Saul, on his way to Damascus to round up more followers, was blinded by a light and fell off his horse. He then heard a voice saying, "Saul, Saul! Why do you persecute me" (Acts 9:4 NIV)? At this point, Jesus identified Himself as the one being persecuted. Soon thereafter, Saul was introduced to a Christian named Ananias. Ananias, instructed by the Lord, placed his hands on Saul and baptized him. It was at that moment that Saul's life was forever changed. Now, as a newly "minted" convert, "He went straight to the synagogues and began to preach that Jesus was the Son of God" (Acts 9:20 GNT).

So, one minute we find Saul hunting down the believers, throwing them into prison to be tortured and/or killed. The next minute, following his encounter with the risen Lord and empowered by the Holy Spirit, he's proclaiming Jesus as the Messiah!

As it turned out, Saul (later called Paul), worked, traveled, and suffered the rest of his life in service of Jesus. By his own admission he says:

> For I am the least of the apostles and do not even deserve to be called an apostle, because I persecuted the church of God. But by the grace of God I am what I am, and His grace to me was not without effect. No, I worked harder than all of them—yet not I, but the grace of God that was with me. Whether, then, it is I or they, this is what we preach, and this is what you believed (1 Corinthians 15:9–11 NIV).

Most conversion stories are not as dramatic. It appears that Jesus knew the apostles would need help—what better witness than the man who tried to stamp out the early Christian movement!

No one ever knows when Jesus will enter into their lives. Most people do not have a "Damascus" experience. God in his infinite wisdom chose to intervene in Saul's case. For the rest of us, Jesus waits patiently without imposing on our free will:

> "Behold, I stand at the door and knock. If anyone hears My voice and opens the door, I will come in and dine with him, and he with Me" (Revelation 3:20 ESV).

The Prodigal Daughter

As long as our hearts are open to his invitation, Jesus will (and does) appear at unexpected times. Such was the case with Leah Darrow, a former model and contestant on *America's Next Top Model*. After reading about her story in a local newspaper, I invited her onto my radio show, "The Business of Living." If ever there was a modern story of "The Prodigal Son," Leah's would be it, only with a change in title: "The Prodigal *Daughter*." Here, I share her story:

Leah was brought up with her five siblings on a farm in Oklahoma. Her parents, devout Catholics, raised their kids in the faith. They attended Mass every week and prayed together as a family. As she entered high school, things began to change, not unlike what many adolescents experience. Peer pressure got the best of her, causing her to make poor decisions, especially with regard to relationships. As Leah describes it, "The pressure from others caused a slow fade." It wasn't as if she didn't think about her relationship with God; she remained curious about her faith. But the slow fade continued into college.

Soon after graduation, the fade would kick into high gear. On a whim, she decided to try out for *America's Next Top Model*. She was chosen as one of the fourteen finalists in season three, but in the third round, she was the second to be cut. Undeterred, she decided to pursue modeling as a full-time career, which brought her to New York. Before long, she started landing modeling jobs.

At one point, an international magazine called her after seeing her on *America's Next Top Model*. They were very impressed and told her they'd like to showcase her in their magazine in a sexy, sultry way. Having been steeped in the modeling culture (e.g., vanity, pride, money, etc.) and enjoying the NYC scene, she accepted the offer. This decision is what would soon lead to what she describes as "a moment of grace—my St. Paul moment." During the photo shoot, the photographer was snapping pictures in rapid fire—over and over. The flashes across her face caused her to start blinking to regain her focus. Chances are you've had a similar experience when temporarily blinded by a light. At this point, I'm going to let Leah tell the rest of the story (as transcribed from the actual interview):

> As I was blinking, I was fully conscious and fully aware. I saw an image of myself in an immodest outfit. (Then) I saw my hands cupped together at my waist and then raising them up all the way up as if I were giving them to someone. I didn't see anything—not God or angels. The only thing I did see at the end was when I raised my hands up—it was a profile of a man's face. A shadowy profile of a man's face looking at my hands at what I was offering and then he bowed his head in disappointment. That's all I saw—that was it. And once I saw that, though, I remember feeling very scared, and I pulled my hands back down to see what was in

them—and they were completely empty. There was nothing in them.

After that, the photographer was saying, "Leah, Leah, come on—stay focused!" I just looked at him and realized—I wasn't quite sure what had happened. I wasn't quite sure what was going on. I realized I wasn't offering anything to God. That everything I was doing in my life, everything was only for me, and I was living a life of the theology of Leah Darrow. Not by the theology of the Roman Catholic Church, which I believe in. I had made adjustments in my life to justify my (poor) behavior, and so, in the moment of the photo shoot, I realized it wasn't just fashion or modeling—it was my whole life. It was totally centered on myself.

I'm sure what happened next completely startled the photographer. She told him she couldn't do it anymore and walked out. She simply walked out of a lucrative photo shoot! She immediately called her dad who drove over 2,000 miles to pick her up and bring her back home. He brought her to church where she reconciled herself with God. As Leah puts it:

It took many years to reformat my life. God has blessed me so much. He's given me the opportunity to work for Him full-time. And so now I've dedicated my life to speaking all over the world— helping people realize their call to holiness and the fact that they can change.

In addition to her speaking, Leah has recently published, *The Other Side of Beauty—Embracing God's Vision for Love and True Worth.*

Many people like Leah were raised with a solid Christian foundation but for various reasons drift away. Some people drift and never come back. Leah never pushed God out of her life—in my estimation, this kept the door open. Jesus saw that the ground was fertile and entered her life in dramatic fashion!

Turning Evil to Good

The year was 1972. Nine-year-old Kim Phuc and her family were living in the Trang Bang, a South Vietnamese village that was being bombed. As they were fleeing, the bombs, which contained napalm, detonated all around them. Napalm is a flammable liquid that literally sticks to your skin. When ignited, it causes horrible burns and essentially melts the skin right off of the bone. In what has become an iconic photo deserving of a Pulitzer Prize, Kim is shown running naked down a road, with a face transmitting anguish, horror, and pain. She had torn her clothes off which were covered with napalm causing severe burns over most of her body.

On the way to the hospital, Phuc thought for sure that she would die. She spent a year in the hospital receiving multiple skin grafts. Given the physical and mental anguish, she didn't want to live. As the years slowly passed, she decided to look to religion to try to make sense out of the tragedy. At age 19, she became a Christian and claimed that it was her newfound faith in God that saved her.

During an interview with Public Radio International's (PRI's) *The World*, Phuc was asked whether she harbors any anger today. She replied:

> Right now, no. But before, yes. Before I held the hatred for a while. And I learned to forgive. I learned to love my enemies. That is from learning. I'm not born with that. I was raised in a different religion. I was raised in a Cao Dai religion

in Vietnam, but I was missing something. And I just wondered, "Where are you, God?" But then finally I went to the library, and I had read so many religious books, and among that, I read the Bible. Then I changed my attitude, changed my behavior.

Further, as she tells it:

When I became Christian, I have a wonderful connection—the relationship between me, and Jesus, and God. I really want to thank God that he spared my life when I was a little girl. Whatever happened to me, I have another opportunity to be alive, to be healthful, to be a blessing, to help honor other people.

As in the case of Louis Zamperini, her commitment to Christ also led her to completely forgive those responsible for her pain and suffering.

Today, Kim is a mother and grandmother living in Toronto. She has established the Kim Foundation, which helps children who are victims of war heal. She is also a UNESCO Goodwill Ambassador for a Culture of Peace.

These are just a few examples of "ordinary" people who have dramatically changed their lives for the better as a result of accepting Jesus Christ and living the Gospel message. They, in turn, have inspired countless others through their witness, changing hearts and winning souls for Christ. We are *all* called to holiness. It is my fervent hope and prayer that if you haven't done so already, commit (or for those who have drifted away recommit) your life to Jesus. Your life will change for the better and for all eternity. As St. Paul tells us, "Therefore, if anyone is in Christ, he is a new creation; old things have passed away; behold, all things have become new" (2 Corinthians 5:17 WEB).

My wish for you is that by surrendering to God, when God calls you home, you are greeted with the following words taken from Matthew's Gospel: "Well done my good and faithful servant" (Matthew 25:21 NLT)!

About the Author

An experienced author and speaker, Scott Ventrella is a high-profile executive coach, business teacher, and Christian leader serving the greater New York metropolitan area. His first book, *The Power of Positive Thinking in Business*, was published by Simon & Schuster in 2001. It met with success in hard and soft cover, as well as audio CD format, and has been published in 24 languages around the world. His latest book about managing your life the same way you would manage a business, *Me, Inc.: How to Master the Business of Being You* (John Wiley & Sons, 2007), was the focus of a feature in *Elle* magazine's January 2005 issue.

Over the past two decades, Ventrella has delivered speeches to management groups and coached top-level executives at major multinational corporations including Constellation Brands, Hess Corporation, IBM, Ogilvy & Mather, PepsiCo, and Verizon. In addition, he has been teaching a life leadership course at Fordham University's Gabelli School of Business in New York City for the past 24 years.

While he is not a theologian or an ordained priest, Ventrella's commitment to his Christian faith runs deep and spans his entire lifetime. He has served as an executive at the Peale Center for Christian Living, coached clergymen from an Episcopal priest to a senior rabbi of a major synagogue, and has served for 30 years as a Catechist working with ninth graders preparing for Confirmation. He has been a featured speaker and workshop presenter at The First Congregational Church, St. Mark's Episcopal, Fairfield Presbyterian, Litchfield First Congregational Church, St. Mary's Catholic Church, and St. Stephen's Episcopal Church.

In addition to serving as an adjunct professor at Fordham University, Ventrella has been teaching at Fairfield University since 2007 and at Sacred Heart University since 2009.